Being an African Student

Stories of Opportunity and Determination

Samson Akinloye Omotosho

UNIVERSITY PRESS OF AMERICA,® INC.

Lanham • Boulder • New York • Toronto • Oxford

Copyright © 2005 by
University Press of America,® Inc.
4501 Forbes Boulevard
Suite 200
Lanham, Maryland 20706
UPA Acquisitions Department (301) 459-3366

PO Box 317
Oxford
OX2 9RU, UK

Library of Congress Control Number: 2004114186

ISBN: 978-0-7618-2991-1

Contents

Preface

This book explores the life world of African students in the U.S. It aims at revealing what the experience is like to be a foreign student, particularly, to be an African student. It intends to provide a deeper understanding of the students' experience and what the experience means to them. It is hoped that such understanding would facilitate the interaction between African students, their counterparts, their faculties and others with whom they relate, making the interaction richer, more meaningful and more productive.

As students, faculty and others who are not Africans gain more understanding of the world of the African students they may encounter clearer insights into their own world as well. After all, in reality, we are not only characters in our own stories but also in the stories of others. Our own stories thus go forward as we act in ways that advance the stories of others.

Using the personal stories of eleven African students and mine, this book seeks to answer such questions as: What is it like for Africans to be students in the U.S. and what is it like for them to detach from their heritage and home places to become students in the U.S.? Being an African student is a phenomenon and the students' stories serve as a lens through which to look at, and understand the phenomenon. As human beings, we are bound to our stories, our memories and our histories. They are the complex intertwining elements of past experiences and feelings of which we are composed. They come into our experiences each day and they help us to recall, asking again, what is a particular experience like for us?

It is hoped that insights uncovered from dialogues and conversations with the students would help make curricula more effective and attentive to the needs of the African students. As the readers listen, they too may begin to see the connection between the students' stories, their own stories and larger stories of culture and humanity.

This book is derived from my doctoral dissertation at the University of Maryland at Baltimore. In doing that work, I discovered that most previous works about foreign students, even though quite informative, were deductively done. This work has adopted a different, inductive approach, attempting to understand the phenomenon directly from the point of view and interpretation of the persons that experienced it.

The book may be of interest to faculty, researchers and student advisors who need to understand the world of African students, the students' difficulties and how best to advice them. It may also be of interest to those who have the responsibility of administering international students and multicultural programs in schools and colleges. Furthermore, I believe the book will be a useful tool anywhere the issues, success and progress of foreign students, particularly African students, are considered important.

Introduction

The need to understand the world of foreign and international students will continue to increase as advancement in communication moves the human race toward a global community. Planners of school curricula will need such understanding to ensure that the teaching-learning community is one of mutual respect and caring, a community in which students from different races, creeds and colors can achieve their optimum potentials. Based on that premise, this book sets out to understand the life world of African students.

The phenomenological approach was used to uncover the meaning of being an African student. The meaning of the experience emerged in the process of dialogues with eleven African students. The students narrated various aspects of their experiences, beliefs and values. From the interpretation of the students' personal stories, deeper meanings, concerns and aspirations of African students were uncovered.

Students sometimes interpreted their experiences differently, depending on their personal situations. Students who had lived in the U.S. prior to entering school had a fairly different experience from those admitted to school directly as they came from Africa. Those who were already familiar with the American school system seemed to experience less need for further adaptation to school. Students who spoke English in their countries of origin experienced a little less difficulty communicating than those who did not. Students whose families were in the U.S. or who lived with their families had different difficulty levels in school experiences. Students who enjoyed financial aid and sponsorships recounted different experiences from those who worked long hours to pay for school. Yet, there were many common and similar trends that cut across the students' experiences, which could be related simply to being from Africa.

Even though the students' goals, values, motivation, hardiness, resilience and capacity for adaptation might vary, sharing in one another's stories allowed for a primal discovery of an embodied knowing in such a way that shared meaning could be captured. Capturing of those common and shared meanings was the objective of this book and the shared meanings, hopefully, will enrich the understanding of the world of African students by others with whom they have to study, work and relate.

Chapter One

Sound of the Knocking Shoes

Nigeria 1958. It was a Saturday morning. I dressed up in my "white-over-khaki" uniform and started for school. My parents did their best to convince me that there was no school but it was all to no avail. My mother took me outside of the house with the hope that, perhaps, the absence of other school children from the streets would dissuade my innocent, school-zealous mind. Even that did not work. I just had to go; I could not afford to miss school. Though I was only six years old and about two months into Elementary One, I had developed a liking for school that was to serve as the foundation for my affinity for learning in later years. Seeing my desperation that morning, my father said to my mother, "Let him go", and my mom did.

School was about thirty minutes away and I always trekked in the company of other pupils. However, that fateful Saturday morning, it was a solitary walk for me. In a little while, my solitude earned a companion; vacillation. I started to doubt my self-conceived sureness about school being open. I kept on going anyway. On getting to the school, I found no single human being. My solitude would have been complete but for birds and crickets etching their beautiful chirpings upon the canvas of an eerie silence.

In orienting to the theme of this book, I recall and reflect on that personal story. It is a story that offers itself as an exemplar of the place of education in the heart of an African child, especially one from the Yoruba tribe. It depicts how strongly and how early in life, the value of education has been impressed upon the mind of the child. Still today, I can hear in my mind many of the sayings and the songs that my mother used to sing as she did her daily chores.

Folk songs, riddles, sayings, stories and proverbs usually teach morals to children in the African culture. One of my mother's favorite songs goes thus:

> Your shoes will sound, 'ko-ko-ka'.
> Your shoes will sound, 'ko-ko-ka'.
> If you study your books,
> Your shoes will sound, 'ko-ko-ka'.

What does education have to do with shoes, one might ask? In the Yoruba post-colonial society, most of those who first became educated also became successful. They no longer did menial jobs. They could afford to dress well and wear nice and expensive shoes. Coincidentally, such shoes in those days were hard-soled, and they knocked, i.e., made the sounds 'ko-ko-ka' as you walked. Soon, knocking shoes not only became a vogue, it became synonymous with being educated! So, right from the soul of the mother, that song represented a wish, a prayer, and an admonishment for her child to take education seriously in order to become 'successful' and respectable.

Mom also had many favorite sayings. One she frequently said to us was: "If you have neither education nor training, get ready to work as a porter." Porters, known as "alaaru" (meaning load carrier) among the Yorubas were found in marketplaces and bus terminals. For a small fee, they transported heavy loads for people, carrying the loads on their heads or backs. Apart from being a slave, an "alaru" could just as well represent the poorest and lowliest thing a person could be, as far as the Yoruba's were concerned.

Songs and sayings as described above are used in a typical Yoruba family to constantly teach and remind the children of cultural values and beliefs. One such belief is that education is the single most effective tool for turning around a life of poverty. In fact, the Yorubas in general pride themselves in the belief that they are one of the most educated and enlightened subgroups among the African people. The great personal value I have for education originated from a family and a tribe that has an equally strong faith in education. And that faith is like a rock!

Using my personal stories and those of eleven other African students, this book, therefore, explores the world of African students to provide insights into such questions as, what is it like to be an African student in the U.S. and what is it like for such students to detach from their heritage and home places in order to study in the U.S.? Being an African student is a phenomenon and the students' stories serve as a lens through which one can look at, and understand that phenomenon. After all, as human beings, we are bound to our stories, our memories and our histories. They are the complex intertwining elements of past experiences and feelings of which we are composed. They come into our experiences each day and they help us to recall and to reconsider what a particular experience is like for us. In telling our personal stories we found meaning rooted in our own experience and in the connection of our stories to those of one another. As you read and listen, you too may begin to see and reconsider the connection between our stories, your own story and larger stories of culture and humanity.

COMING TO AMERICA

When, in 1991, a friend offered me the possibility of coming to America, I was excited about the economic prospects of the offer. I saw it as an opportunity to fulfill my ambition of earning a doctoral degree in nursing. No university in Nigeria was offering a doctorate in nursing at that time. For me, earning a doctoral degree was one of the means for becoming the best of what I was. It was a move toward making the best of my nursing career. I knew also that it would afford me the opportunity to be more useful and helpful to my family as well as to many members of my extended family.

For me, being an African student in the U.S. is, therefore, pursuing a life goal and a dream. It is taking up a venture into which it is worth putting everything. It is plunging into the unknown with all its anxiety; all for the sake of what that venture is worth. It is an experience upon which many hopes and aspirations are contingent. But that is for me. I wonder what it is for others. I wonder what personal, familial, social, and cultural values brought other Africans to the U.S. to study? I wonder how much pressure they are under, being African students? What keeps them going in spite of the hardships they encounter? I ask myself as I reflect about my own aspirations, what hopes and dreams interplay inside the world of African students and how do they go about achieving their dreams and aspirations?

I saw the movie, "Coming to America" starring Eddie Murphy and Arsenio Hall in August 1991, just two weeks after I came to the U.S. One of the themes of the movie that stood out for me was that of damning the costs of realizing a dream. I recognized the theme because it resonated well with my own experience of coming to America. The dream of Akeem (played by Eddie Murphy in the movie) was to come and find a wife in America who could effectively engage him in intellectual discourse. This was in opposition to marrying an African lady whom the king, Akeem's father, wanted him to take, but whom Akeem saw as too servile and too submissive for his liking. After all, as the whole world believes, America is the land of opportunities; what can't you find in America?

So, to America the two friends came, fixing their eyes on that single mission of finding a wife with intellect, while they damned all the costs that attended the mission. Some of the costs for Akeem were the loss of the luxury and comfort of his father's palace. He knew he would have to forfeit the pomp and pageantry of a royal wedding. He would have to exchange the familiarity and security of home for the anxiety of an unknown and strange land. Everything was worth his dream, including the perils, assault and robbery he experienced in downtown Manhattan and the outright relegation of 'prince Akeem' to the level of a common man by New Yorkers to whom the idea of 'king' or 'prince' meant next to nothing.

Similarly, my coming to the U.S. was an experience laden with a lot of anxiety and obstacles right from day one. If not because of what the coming meant to me, I probably would have abandoned the venture in its very infancy. Take for instance my experience with securing a U.S. visa. In order to do that I had to pass the Commission on Graduates of Foreign Nursing Schools exam (CGFNS), an exam only well known for the fact that people seldom passed it. The exam was not being administered in Nigeria, thus I had to go to Liberia to take it. Liberia is six countries west of Nigeria. At the time I went there to sit for the CGFNS exam, the war in Liberia was just beginning. This made the roads more perilous, especially for strangers traveling the African West Coast.

I needed about 6,000 Naira (then, $300) to make the journey but my salary was only 9,600 Naira per annum. So, not only did I risk spending all my savings, I had to borrow additional money for the journey. That meant putting on hold all of my other commitments and family responsibilities. My exam permit did not arrive from the U.S. until the day before the exam. I became increasingly anxious as I waited. As expensive as it was in Nigeria, I had to send several fax messages to the CGFNS office in Pennsylvania. I could not buy my traveling ticket to Liberia or make other traveling arrangements, as I was not sure if the permit would arrive. Everyday, I looked anxiously for the mail. By the time the permit came, I had less than half a day to get many things done. I had to buy the flight ticket and travel to Lagos Airport (200 miles away) in order to confirm the ticket. Liberia was four hours by air from Nigeria. I would also have to locate the exam hall when I got to the strange and busy city of Monrovia. I was in a state of panic!

Somehow I managed to get to Liberia and found the exam hall. As if the past tension was not enough, the examining officer surprised me by saying that I could not sit for the exam because my name was not on "the master list." That was devastating to say the least. What would that mean? So many questions ran across my mind in quick succession. Was that the end of my dream? That would be immensely frustrating. Would I go back to Nigeria and tell my friends and family I was disallowed to take an exam for which I had prepared so much? That would be ridiculous. Would I have the will to repeat this journey? Unthinkable!

I went back to Nigeria by road (a five-day journey), as I did not have enough money to buy a return ticket. We were stopped day and night and sometimes harassed by soldiers at more than twenty army checkpoints that were mounted because of the impending war. It was the longest, most dangerous and most tedious journey I have ever taken in my life. I reported my ordeal to the CGFNS in writing. They sent me an apology and a check to cover all my expenses. That was as amazing as it was comforting. The money helped to offset some of my debts. More importantly, the CGFNS response was a gesture that soothed my soreness from the futility of that Liberia trip. It was a thoughtful, caring, and prompt response that further fueled my love, respect, and interest in coming to America.

I went to sit for the exam in Ghana a couple of months later, passed and got a U.S. visa, but the memory of the ordeal I endured lingers on. For me, the perseverance of the Liberia experience is one of the stories that depicts the price and meaning of being an African student. As I reflect on my own experience, I wonder what other African students endure and sacrifice in order to come here and what the coming means to them? What have they invested in their journey? What does being an African student mean when the price and the personal sacrifices of coming, staying, and studying in the U.S. are put into consideration?

LEARNING TO SPEAK 'RIGHT'

Africa is a multi-ethnic and multi-linguistic continent. Nigeria alone comprises over 200 ethnic and sub-ethnic groups and over 200 local dialects. It comprises 3 main tribes and languages and 3 major religions. I spent my first 2 years of elementary school life in one of Nigeria's most tribally heterogeneous cities, Lokoja. The only way by which people communicated in the schools in such a State was to speak the common official language, English. By the time my parents moved back to our own State, I had developed an appreciable level of proficiency in speaking the English language, even though, in my own State, we were free to speak in our tribal language, Yoruba. Since people felt more at ease speaking in their mother tongue, my new classmates, in my home State, interacted usually in Yoruba and could not be said to be nearly as proficient in English as I was. So, in terms of speaking in English, I became the 'one-eye king in the city of the blind'.

The skill thus became a quality of pride for me. It helped me tremendously in understanding other subjects. It earned me respect in the school: it was rare to find an elementary school pupil who could speak English as fluently as I did. Word went around the entire school so quickly that I soon became one of the centers of attraction at lunch breaks. In fact, there was a particular teacher in the school who would invite me to talk to him in English and then reward me with money with which I usually treated myself to some extra lunch. Often, while I conversed with this teacher in English, other teachers and pupils stood by, watching, I guess, in amazement. My English language skill not only enhanced my learning up through college, it gave earned me considerable attention and admiration from others. I was proud of myself too!

Once in the U.S., I had to reconsider that impression of self. Most especially because of the difference in accents, I had to relearn communicating in English. As I tried and sometimes strained to understand what my teachers or classmates or patients were saying, I noticed that they too frequently did the same in trying to understand me. Many have told me, sometimes directly and sometimes in the form of a compliment, that I spoke with an accent, or even "with a heavy accent." I, who spoke English in my first and second elementary schools without with considerable admiration from others, now found comprehending and being comprehended a difficult task.

This represents one of the many instances of how the African students' experience of self alters with change in social and cultural contexts. I wonder how other students' experiences of self have changed or have been altered by being in the U.S. How have they experienced relearning to communicate in English, learning new ways of dressing relative to the weather and social functions and learning new cultural values, social norms or ways of behaving, especially with their classmates and teachers? In short, what is it like for the African students to experience various aspects of themselves in different lights due to change in social and cultural context? What is the experience like for students who come from non-English speaking African countries such as Togo, Dahomey, the Ivory Coast, or the Cameroons? How do they communicate or relearn to communicate in the U.S.?

BETWEEN SYMPATHY AND EMPATHY

My first place of work when I came to the U.S. was Harlem Hospital Center, Harlem, New York. I worked as a registered nurse on a kidney floor. One of the first patients I took care of was a young adult male who used cocaine and other drugs and was at the terminal stages of full blown AIDS and renal failure. He frequently lamented the sad story of his life and the constant recurrence of his pain. While I stood by his bedside listening to him one day, it occurred to me that he was anxious about the reality of his imminent death. So, I verbally expressed sympathy for him, as I would have done in a Nigerian context. Suddenly, this patient snapped at me saying, "Cut it out Man, do something Man!" That jolted me back into the awareness that I was in a U.S. hospital. It also gave me the first inkling that the nursing setting in Nigeria allowed for a more open expression of sympathy than my new nursing subculture did.

From that initial "cut-it-out" experience, I began to think that as an African nursing student, I would have to reconsider my previous professional roles, expectations and values in the light of those of American clients. I wonder how other African students adjust to the incongruence between their perceived social and professional roles and the American expectations of those roles. Have they had to give up one for the other? Or, do they find an in between position for themselves? What is it like for a student to make such an adjustment?

BETWEEN COURTESY AND BOLDNESS

Two years later, I was teaching a clinical lab class as a teaching assistant in my doctoral program. One of the students was giving a repeat performance of some procedure I had earlier demonstrated to the class. As her colleagues and I watched, she was doing the procedure wrongly. Spontaneously, I said to her, "What are you doing?" Looking straight back at me, she replied, "What do you think I'm doing?" That response gave me a shock that I did not allow to show in my face. It reminded me in a flash that this was America. The student probably saw my question as challenging or confrontational and so, she responded defensively rather than reflectively.

Within a typical Nigerian context, it was not likely that a student would react to a teacher that way. The intention of the teacher would have been to call the student to, at least, a momentary reflection on the appropriateness or inappropriateness of what she was doing. This student's response, coming from a student to a teacher, would have been seen as abominable, even if the student was older in age than the teacher. In the first place, you did not look a teacher, a senior, or an older person straight in the eye while talking to them. That would have been equally as discourteous as the response itself. During the episode, I thought the student's behavior was only an extension of the boldness that characterized American studentship. However, I later learned from an American professor that, even within the American cultural context, that student's behavior was rude.

As an African student in America, I had to start recognizing the mutual respect, boldness, and assertiveness that characterized the teacher-student relationship rather than the student to teacher courteousness that I had been accustomed to in Nigeria. I had gradually overcome some of the discomfort and inner conflict that I felt in learning to look a teacher straight in the eye or in calling them by their first names. For me, that, and other similar transitions, represented a tremendous cultural shift laden with a gnawing unease. I wonder what the experience is like for other African students. How do they make similar transitions and in what direction? How have they been able to reconcile the level of courteousness previously learned with the new call to boldness, assertiveness and confidence?

BETWEEN DEPTH AND BREADTH

The first time I sat for the U.S. Registered Nurse Licensing Exam, I failed. Later, when preparing to retake the exam, I attended a review course and passed the exam. In that review, I learned the extremely wide spectrum of facts that students needed to know in order to pass nursing exams. I also discovered some fundamental differences between the educational and study approaches I had been used to, and those that characterized the American educational system. I concluded from the experience that, while the student in Nigeria needed to know clinical conditions in depth and must be able to explain each condition in detail, students in the U.S. must learn to make judgments and decisions about a broad range of clinical problems. The comparison, therefore, is a case of depth versus breadth and that of explanation versus judgment.

The challenge in this experience is not about choosing which educational mindset to develop. Rather, it is in how the African student might adapt to the American curricular orientation using skills developed within an African context. How do the students reconcile the two emphases in their learning and practice? How does a study habit whose focus is depth and explanation enhance or impair learning within a different curricular focus? What is the experience like for the African students to learn within the American curricular context?

TECHNOLOGY: DILEMMA OR BLESSING?

Profuse technology and information in the U.S. were two things that amazed and distressed me at the same time. Life was constantly figuring things out. For some, this ranged from vending machines to elevator buttons, from variety of door handles to variety of water taps. As an African student, however, learning to integrate the computer into my schoolwork was my greatest challenge. It was very stressful to learn to type and to do statistics and other class assignments, using the computer.

In my first statistics class, the teacher gave at least one computer assignment per week. As my classmates raced eagerly to the computer lab to get their assignments done, I quietly and sometimes dejectedly took mine home. I felt left out of what looked like an exciting experience that probably could have made my learning easier. I sat up all night on occasions, manually battling assignments and finally submitting them, handwritten. Though I did most of the work well and the content of each product was essentially appropriate, a teacher soon spotted my dilemma, called me and explained why I must, and how I should, learn to use the computer. I observed that Korean, Chinese, and other Asian students did not seem to experience the same difficulty that I did. They usually hurried to the computer lab to do their assignments with enthusiasm similar to that of their American counterparts.

I therefore wonder what it is like for other African students to feel left out of the 'technological race' in the learning and work settings. What is it like for African students to use or not to use the computer and other forms of technology in their learning? What is the effect of the experience on them personally, academically or professionally?

Eventually, a classmate of mine saw my ordeal and volunteered to literally sit by me for a few minutes at the computer lab for the next few weeks to teach me the basic computer. We were the only males in the class; he was Caucasian and American and I was African. My proficiency and confidence in using the computer gradually increased. This made my schoolwork easier. Yet, I wonder what the need to learn and use the computer and other technology is like for other African students. What danger was present for the African self to become technologically minded? What is it like to leave a culture that is more in tune with nature than it is to modern technology and adapt to a new culture where one is bombarded by the presence and the call to the use of modern technology?

THE 'AFRICAN TIME'

Two semesters into my doctoral program I took a course co-taught by two professors. They both invited me for a talk in one of their offices at the end of one of their classes. At the meeting they counseled me regarding my tardiness in coming to class and in submitting assignments. I explained my reasons for my frequent lateness. Or, were they excuses? The professors showed understanding but one of them warned, "Listen, you cannot guaranty that later Pharaohs will be favorable to Joseph."

However, some months later, I needed a participant for an interview and a colleague of mine found one for me. She arranged for us to meet. However, she had told the man that he would find me "to be a nice guy," but that I would "definitely come late for appointments." And, truly I did! When I met the man and started to apologize, he said, "You don't have to apologize, I have already been told that you are a nice guy, but that you would surely come late. That's O.K. Let's get down to business." From that response I got back a painful mirror image of my social self. It was one of the experiences that made me take the fact more seriously that in America, not only official business such as a lecture enjoys strict scheduling; social life is equally highly programmed. Dinners, parties, picnics and visits do not just happen. They are thoroughly scheduled operations. Sociability is not usually improvised; it is very programmatic and predictable.

It took me some effort to adjust to a different regard for time. This was partly because I had been used to the more leisurely orientation to 'African time' and partly because of my own poor time management. African culture is relatively informal and tolerates more latitude around schedules. In America, I have walked into the offices of many a teacher without an appointment. On some occasions the professors could be in the middle of some activity or even on their way out of the office, so that they could not meet with me conveniently. As I increasingly realized the disruption this habit was causing everyone concerned, including myself, I made an effort to improve my use and planning of time. I wonder what other African students have experienced about use and management of time and what changes they have had to make. What is it like for the students to make that change?

Chapter Two

The African Students

You are invited to meet the eleven African students who have shared their experiences with me in this book. All of their names have been replaced with pseudonyms. Some of the pseudonyms had meanings relevant to the students' situations, following the African practice of naming people according to their respective prevailing circumstances. The introduction of the students at this point provides a glimpse into the characters of the very individuals who lived the stories that form this book.

SHEILA

Sheila was a 32-year old African student from Nigeria who was in the final year of her B.S. Nursing degree program. She was a very articulate and friendly person. She had been in the U.S. since 1988 to join her spouse who was also a Nigerian and a physical therapist. She already had a B.S. Agriculture degree from a Nigerian university. Sheila had chosen nursing as a career partly because her spouse liked it and partly because, as she said, "nurses were well respected and well paid."

Sheila missed the opportunity to participate actively in the student organization. She remembered how well she performed as the president of the student union of her university in Nigeria. She remarked, "Now I am not having much fun because I work so many jobs in order to have enough money to send to my parents and sister back home."

RUTH

Ruth was a 45-year old woman from South Africa who was in the final year of her Ph.D. program at the time of this study. She struck me as a very thoughtful person. She was also very humorous. She received her B.S. nursing degree in South Africa and the M.S. degree at the University of California.

Ruth worked as a clinical nurse in a critical care unit. She hoped to return to South Africa as soon as she finished her Ph.D. program because, she said, "we need leaders back home". Thus, she would like to help fulfill the needs of her country that had sacrificed so much to send her to school.

BEN

Ben was a 38-year old man from Nigeria. He was a registered nurse in Nigeria before he came to the U.S. in 1991. He failed the R.N. board examination three times because he was not used to the American system of examination and the objective test. He recalled, "I passed after reading about five different review books, and attending three review courses." Since then, he had been working as a psychiatric nurse. He was bitter about the fact that people said he spoke with an accent and so they could not understand him. However, he was happy that many professors were helpful to him in his current B.S. degree program.

SANDRA

Sandra was a 35-year old African student who had been a registered nurse, a midwife, and a community health nurse in Malawi before coming to America. She went to Northern Ireland for her B.S. degree in nursing and came to the U.S. for her M.S. degree. She left two sons behind with her mother and sister when she came to the U.S. Though the younger son was just fourteen months old by the time she was leaving, she did not feel uncomfortable leaving him because the baby would be taken care of, the reason being that "There is a very strong family tie and a sense of mutual obligation to one another in my family."

Sandra believed that African students in the U.S., including herself, were bi-cultural; they keep some of their African cultural beliefs as they transition into the American culture. For her, "it was like living in-between or crossing cultures."

Sandra became a nurse because it had been her childhood dream. She also loved teaching but she could not clearly explain how she developed interest in teaching. She thought it was probably because her father was also a teacher. She hoped to go back to Malawi to teach after completing her M.S. degree.

EDNA

Edna was a 34-year old African student from Swaziland. Though both of her parents were uneducated, they wanted her to get her education and to be a teacher. She however, wanted to be a nurse, being motivated by her aunt who was a nurse. So, when her father gave her the fee to register into a teachers' college, she "sneaked over to nursing school and put in an application there." She said she had to lie to her father that she had to go and look for other options when the school of education did not offer her an admission.

Edna, like Sandra, left her son at home in Africa, in the care of her cousin; she remarked that her family ties were "very strong and dependable." Relationships "are very tight," and "there are no distant relatives; it is embarrassing to call a relative, a distant relative," she remarked.

Edna was a registered nurse, a midwife, and a community health nurse. She held a B.S. degree in nursing and a Master's in community health. She was surprised that, as a foreign student, you had to fend for yourself, including finding accommodation. Though she found such experiences very difficult, she remarked that the difficulties later "helped me to grow and to be independent".

ABEKE

Abeke was a 24-year old student from Nigeria. "Abeke" is a Yoruba name that means "someone that others love to pamper." Though agreeable to the name, the student burst into laughter when I suggested it as her pseudonym. I gave her that name because, by induction from her personal stories, she was a pampered child. Shortly after graduating from high school, Abeke's father gave her, as a gift, an airline ticket to come to the U.S. and continue her studies. Though her father thought he was giving his daughter a token of love and a pleasant surprise, she had mixed emotions about the gift. She said, "I had been looking forward to having fun and having a blast with my friends in one of the universities in Nigeria." While Abeke was the only one of the eleven students who neither planned nor desired to come to the U.S., she came anyway.

Abeke was a young, vibrant and articulate woman. She expressed herself clearly and confidently. She had a very good sense of humor and talked intelligently. As she was only 19 years old when she left Africa, it was frightening for her "to imagine traveling alone to a distant and strange country." It was equally frightening to see her self literally walking away from the cozy enclave of a supportive extended family to a foreign land where she neither knew, nor was known by anyone.

It was so difficult for Abeke and her family to part the day she was leaving Nigeria. She said, "At the airport, we were all so busy talking, hugging, laughing and crying that we didn't hear the boarding announcement. So, I missed my flight and had to travel the following day."

Abeke was in the second year of her B.S. program during the time of this dialogue with her. She had taken two years of prerequisite courses in a county community college prior to coming to the present school and program. She had worked as a nursing assistant when she first came to the U.S. That was where she was first impressed by the nurses and decided to become a nurse. She said she was doing quite well in her studies and was "determined to persevere to the end." Abeke got married in the U.S. to another Nigerian, a man whom she described as very supportive.

BIOLA

Biola was a 35-year old lady from Nigeria. She was a classmate and friend of Abeke's. Her pseudonym is an African name that means 'born into wealth,' deriving from the fact that she came from a wealthy family. She had lived and studied in many countries in Europe, including Austria and Denmark before coming to the U.S. After receiving a bachelor's degree in economics in Denmark, she came to the U.S. in 1989 to complete a master's program, make some money and return to Africa. When her B.S. degree did not help her obtain a good job, she decided to change careers. Having lived with, and taken care of her 89-year old grandmother in the past, Biola readily saw nursing as a good career alternative.

Biola took the prerequisites for the associate degree (AA) program but ended up on an indefinite waiting list. She became frustrated and headed for the Licensed Practical Nursing (LPN) School, hoping that by the time she completed that program, the AA school would accept her. She was wrong. She therefore decided to take more prerequisite courses to qualify for the B.S. program. Luckily, she said, in 1996, she was admitted to the B.S. program; she was very happy.

Biola talked freely about her experience. She communicated well in English but frequently had difficulty finding the right word to express a particular idea. She lived with her husband and four children ages 14, 10, 7 and 1. Her family continually encouraged her to go on with the program. Her 14 year old daughter helped her to type school work. She remarked, "I am grateful to God who gave me all the courage I needed to do all I was able to do."

BINU

Binu was a 41-year old man from Ghana. His dream had been to become a neurosurgeon. Unfortunately, shortly after completing high school, his father died. His family then faced serious financial problems and his original dream died. He therefore ended up studying philosophy and psychology in a university in Ghana. He was excited when, in 1991, he got "the opportunity to come to the U.S." He saw it as a chance to revive the dream once again of becoming a neurosurgeon. After all, he said, "The U.S. is the citadel of knowledge, particularly in science and medicine." However, he soon realized that he would not be able to meet the financial demand of medical school and so he decided to take up nursing. He had two semesters to complete the B.S. program at the time of this dialogue with him.

The pseudonym "Binu" means, "To be angry." The countenance of this student throughout our conversation sessions was one of anger. He seemed very embittered and talked most of the time of being "victimized," "betrayed," "frustrated," "angry," "demoralized," "discriminated against," "harassed," "tortured," and "humiliated."

Binu had very high self-esteem. He was proud of his B.S. degree in philosophy-psychology, and proud of how knowledgeable he believed he was. He frequently questioned, or even criticized, most situations or ideas. This, he said, got him into trouble with teachers. He told the story of how he was kicked out of the school for one semester because he "questioned the essence of the life support machine" in one of his clinical rotations. He was very bitter about this experience. He said he thought the teacher would bring the question up for class discussion but instead, "the teacher used it against me, saying that I held a philosophy that was unsafe for the patient." He told the teacher that she was mistaking "opinion" for "philosophy" and proceeded to define the differences between the two to the teacher. On another occasion he told a teacher that she was using a Socratic method of teaching. When the teacher replied that she doubted that Binu knew what "Socratic method" meant, he felt slighted, saying about himself, "This is a guy who has a first

degree in philosophy and psychology, and I would not understand what Socratic method meant? That's an insult to my intelligence. I know Socrates; I
know Plato; I know Aristotle; I know all those people. I know Kant and
Berkely and Freud and Hume!" In a class assignment, another teacher marked
wrong some of the items on Binu's list of the side effects of a particular med-
ication. In reacting, Binu took five textbooks to the teacher's office the following day to prove that he was right.

DAYO

Dayo was a 28-year old lady from Uganda. Dayo meant, "The dawn of hap-
piness." She had just completed her B.S. program and "beginning to
straighten out from the pressure of school." At that point in her experience,
she exclaimed, "I am so happy it's all over! At last, I have time to eat good
food!"

Dayo was a very humorous person and a brilliant student. She had a good
command of the English language and she articulated her ideas very well.
Dayo primarily came to the U.S. ten years earlier to join her boyfriend who
was now her husband and a medical doctor. She held a B.S. degree in Business Administration from the American University in Kenya. There, she was
exposed to some aspects of the American system of education, particularly
conducting literature searches and using the computer. A difference, however,
was that students in Kenya and Uganda were evaluated mainly by essay
rather than multiple-choice questions. She had also completed an M.B.A. degree here in the U.S. before going to nursing school.

Dayo had "a rough childhood." Her mother sewed house curtains for sale
to provide her and four other siblings with just one meal a day. Most of her
mother's income went to paying the children's school tuition. Trying to teach
her children to endure and delay gratification, Dayo's mother urged them to
"always look at the bigger picture of things." Dayo went through her entire
first semester school buying only one textbook, and through the entire B.S.
program having only three. She could not afford any more than that. Otherwise she would not have been able to pay her tuition. "However, in spite of
the hardship," she said, "I did not fail a single course."

ENIOLA

Eniola was a 38-year old Nigerian woman. She came to the U.S. in 1991 having qualified as a registered nurse and having also passed the commission on

graduates of foreign nursing schools (CGFNS) exam. She has since worked as an ER nurse first in New York and now in Baltimore. "Eniola" means, "one with majesty," referring to the respectable and dignified way she talked and carried herself.

Eniola's family came to join her in the U.S. in 1994. Her husband was a medical doctor and was currently studying to pass the medical board exam. In addition to going to school, Eniola worked to sustain her family of five. Eniola began the B.S. nursing program in 1994 and in 1996 converted to the R.N.-to-M.S. track. She communicates fluently and makes her points very clearly. She readily passed as someone with a very high sense of responsibility.

FUNMI

Funmi was a 27-year old lady from the Cameroon's. Her pseudonym was short form for "Gift from the Lord" and derived from the elaborate emphasis she put on her belief that she and her husband "are simply given as gifts to each other by God." She said she and her husband gave each other love and unflinching support. She came from the Cameroon's, a West African country where she said about 80% of the people spoke French and about 20%, English, in addition to the indigenous languages. She came from a tribe that spoke English even though she "learned both languages in school as the law required." In 1990 she had the options of traveling to Britain, Nigeria, Italy, or the U.S. She had relatives in each of those countries but she chose to come to the U.S., "just to try something different." She believed America would best provide the type of experience she wanted.

Funmi held a degree in Accounting only because her parents wanted her to be an accountant. Following that, she felt free to pursue her own interest, a caring profession such as medicine or nursing. She believed she developed that interest from growing up in "a family that is caring and always there for you." She decided to study nursing and took the prerequisite courses at a community college. She started the B.S. program part time because she had just had her second baby. Later, she converted to full time student status.

Funmi's stories were replete with moments of determination not to allow anything to distract her from her pursuits and desires. She was very hopeful and remarked several times about how supportive her husband had been to her.

Chapter Three

Leaving Home
and Becoming a Stranger

Once African students are in the U.S. and especially in their earlier years of living in the U.S., most of their further experiences revolved around a central organizing theme; that of being a stranger. The word 'stranger' has its etymologic root in an old French word, "estrange," which means unusual; odd; unaccountable; not accustomed; or arousing wonder or astonishment. African students described situations in which they felt odd and out of place. They described experiences to which they were not accustomed and narrated personal stories of challenges, wonder, astonishment and determination.

DETACHING FROM HOME

Being an African student in the U.S. began with leaving home. With the exception of Biola, who worked and studied in Europe and came to the U.S. from there, all the other ten students came directly to the U.S. from their home countries. There was, therefore, no way of fully understanding the students' experience without being called to ponder and reflect upon what both home and leaving home meant for the students.

Abeke narrated the story of her leaving home. Hers was the most vivid and emotionally intense experience of leaving home perhaps because she was the youngest, being only nineteen. She said everybody was there to see her off: her parents, brother, sister, aunt, uncle and some of her cousins. There must have been over a dozen of them. "It was like, O God, we are not going to see her forever," she said. So, everyone wanted to be there. She cried, her mom cried, her dad cried. She ended up not leaving Nigeria the day she was supposed to, because, she said, "At the airport, I was sitting with my dad, and he wouldn't let me go, and my mom was sitting right there, and everyone was like, would you two let her go or something? And my parents would say, 'Oh, we are still looking at her because we are not going to see her for a long time, and this and that.'" She ended up missing her flight that night because they sat right there at the airport and didn't hear the boarding announcement. "My luggage went but I did not go anywhere that night. We were so busy talking, hugging, crying and looking at one another's face that we didn't hear the flight announcement!" She recalled with an air of satisfaction.

Abeke's story speaks to many themes that relate to being attached to, and then, detached from home. The presence of so many family and extended family members at the airport spoke to community, concern, and caring. I experienced a similar presence of many family members at my departure from home in 1991. The African life is one of community both in being and in separating. Everyone wanted to show that they cared and that they were concerned about you. Being present at your departure was one way of caring and showing that they cared.

The detachment from home and family was a painful experience. In Abeke's story, the pain, meaning and significance of detachment were embodied and expressed in 'talking, hugging, crying and looking at one another's face'. The face is the threshold to another's being. It beckons, making a claim on us and inviting us into the other's being. At separation, therefore, the student and her family members renewed their claim and responsibility for one another's caring. It is the face of the other that compels one to make a claim and response that originate and sustain a relationship that is ethically caring. Even after two people are physically separated, the impression of their faces in each other's mind continues to make that claim and call for a caring response from each other.

Leaving home meant the breaking of family ties, at least, temporarily and in terms of physical separation. 'Being' then became a kind of detachment; a detachment from home that was laden with mixed emotions for both the students and their families. Abeke further recalled that missing of the flight was good in part because she got to spend another day with her family. The crying, basically, for her parents, she thought, was a cry of joy and a cry of sadness at the same time because they were happy that their child was going abroad to continue her studies but they were sad because they were going to miss part of their being.

The detachment experienced was not only in the sense of separation from family members but from everything that constituted home and the student's relationality to it. Ruth said that sometimes she could not stop thinking of her sisters, nieces and nephews. She said, "It's a terrible thing to be away from home. I miss even the stones and rocks and mountains that I didn't use to care about. We have a lot of them. They are bare mountains. They are rough and ragged. Yet, now I miss them."

Ruth's experience described above reveals the African's strong sense of bond and connection to place, nature, home and family. Even though she had once taken those elements for granted, being detached from them seemed to renew and strengthen her sense of connection to them. For Ruth, the detachment from home was like losing, leaving, and letting go of a paradise. Home is where we experience a sense of harmony, wholeness, unbreakable safety and unconditional love. Once detached from home, the student's sense of harmony seems irretrievably torn apart. As Ruth lamented on the separation, she seemed to yearn to recapture the connection of that paradise lost. Her comment reveals a sense of harmonious oneness with Mother Nature. She, like most Africans, seemed to find solace and joy not only in seeing nature but also in being one with her. What do we give up when we leave our place of birth—our taproot to mother earth? What do the African students know about this experience that others do not know? What needs to be revealed about separation from the place called home? Could their present places of abode become home in the same sense as their African homes?

Home was not just a physical place in African students' lives; it was a significant part of their being. It was a place whose smells, sounds and entire sensual experience they honor. The uniqueness of that experience made it more than just a physical place. They had such a strong sense of attachment to home that one wonders how they came to allow themselves to be detached from it. For them, home was so textual that they told and retold about it to other persons. They seemed to judge their present encounters nostalgically against the texture of the home they left behind.

For African students, texture of home was family and extended family. For the African, particularly the Yoruba's, deep ties to home were sources of strength. They included not only the love and unconditional acceptance by the family but also, according to Ruth, a familiarity and attachment to the inanimate aspects of it such as the rocks, mountains and the blue skies that woke up to see every. The texture of home is exclusive to home. Departures and arrivals emotionally mark the boundaries of home and for most Africans; attachment to home is an integral part of an authentic life.

THE PAINS AND GAINS OF DETACHMENT

There is something painful about being detached from home. Abeke said that she, her father and her mother cried on her departure from home. Sandra recalled that, "It was very difficult to leave home when you are so much part of a very close family." The pains of detachment from home seem to be related to the loss of the familiar and the predictable. Better home than the unknown, the unpredictable, with a stranger imposing strange ways. The pain may also be related to our primordial sense of the need for security, of being held and of belonging.

Granted that leaving home is painful or disruptive; one wonders what lured or pushed people out of the comfort and security of their homes? For the African student, it seemed to be the recognition of the need for a change in their lives and, for one reason or the other, leaving home, a crucial form of detachment, was what would make that change happen. Ruth, for example said "I missed home a lot, but I've got to finish [my studies]; we need leaders back home." She would rather bear the pain of the detachment in exchange for becoming a leader who would eventually go back to serve her home country.

Detachment is at the heart of education and thus, of our ability to think of a better world. The students thus left their homes as they sought a different way of being. They remarked that they missed home, but they would rather bear the pain of detachment that held possibilities for their desired way of being. They seemed to recognize the paradox that many times humans needed to leave their comfort zones in order to experience growth. It probably would be an illusion that all would have been well if we could have just stayed home. In fact, detachment from home can be likened to "separating," a process considered essential in the turning of ordinary materials into gold. However, I wonder if all the students plan to eventually return home? What motivates such plan? What facilitates or hinders it? What happens, when return is not possible or not part of the plan?

GRIEVING THE DETACHMENT

While students narrated their stories, many times they referred to their home countries and what the same experience would have been like, were they home. They talked so passionately about their countries that I wondered if their experiences did not go beyond nostalgia. It seemed to border on grieving, grieving the loss of part of their being. Dayo, for example, said she had difficulty trying to shift from the way things were done back home to the way things were done here. "If somebody has a fever, you mix up a couple of herbs for them to drink, and the fever is gone. You didn't have to know the reason why the herb worked. Now I'm going to have to find a way of doing things that I can explain. If I can't explain it, I can't just do it," she lamented. The detachment that is being grieved here is therefore not only the physical separation from home but also a gradual departure from a familiar culture and way of being.

When the students talked about "being lonely" or "missing my family," or "missing my parents," it was much more in the sense of missing the ones who listened and helped. It meant more than the mere fact that they were alone in the U.S. by themselves. In most instances the people they missed included their extended families, the ones who birthed them, allowed them to be, and supported their continued well being and existence. Biola, for instance, said, "I talk to my family about once a month. I miss them a lot... Sometimes I say 'God, I wish my parents were here. They would have helped take care of my kids.'" Similarly, Funmi remarked, "My parents are in the Cameroon's. I miss them a lot. For the past two weeks, I have been trying to get through to mom; I can't because the line would not go through." Abeke identified one of the ways in which she missed home. She remembered how she could take any problem to family members and "they would at least sit down and listen." But here, she said, "Everyone is busy with life and with their own problems. So you can't even go to someone and start babbling about your own problems. If they even listen at all, they might tell you their own problems and then, you will probably feel like, O.K. maybe mine ain't as bad."

African students continue to maintain strong relations with friends, families and extended families they left back in Africa. Family bonds are so strong that the students being here is like leaving part of themselves back in their home countries. They described how much they missed their families and how frequently they phoned them. African students spend a lot of money on international phone calls to families in Africa. I once spent eight hundred dollars on a telephone bill trying to keep in touch with a family member who was undergoing surgery back home. The grieving experienced by the students from detaching from home was therefore a result of the loss of the comfort, security and pleasure of their home places.

Chapter Four

Being in the U.S.

What being in the U.S. and being in a foreign place really meant to the individual students ranged from cultural shock to an exciting adventure. Abeke described her initial anxiety as arising from the fact that she knew very little about America. She felt quite lonely. She remarked, "Here it's just my self alone. . . . I've never been away from my family." Biola illuminated this experience further when she said; "The social system here focuses on the nuclear family whereas, back home, you have the extended family with you."

In contrast, Eniola seemed to have better prepared her mind for the strangeness. She said that no amount of preparation could get you fully ready for what you will meet in any foreign place thousands of miles away from home but "at least you should expect things are not going to be exactly the same as they were home." She succinctly summarized the views of the other students. She said, "It has been exciting, probably somewhat strange in some areas, but that is not to be unexpected, because this is a foreign land, foreign people, foreign everything. It is a different culture." She however took a fairly more mature and balanced outlook to the entire experience when she remarked: "Although you knew things were not going to be the same, you were not going to eat the same food, mingle with the same kind of people, operate under the situation that you have been used to, you would still feel some aspects of the cultural shock." She gave some examples: "You try to order food and you don't even know what name to call it, you don't know what they call their own cabs, should you call it a cab or a taxi? Should you wear red on Sunday or purple? Is it the restroom or bathroom, the john or ladies. . . . No one can be absolutely ready for life in an unfamiliar place."

The African students' experience of the foreignness of the U.S. to them seemed to add varying degrees of anxiety and excitement to their lives. It all seemed to depend on how well each student anticipated and prepared to make the best of what the foreign place had to offer. The word 'foreign' itself derives from the Latin word, "foramus," which means to be alienated, incongruent, or not connected, This etymological understanding suggest that the student probably felt a sense of alienation and non-connection. Yet, the pedagogy of place reminds us that, as a species, we require a ground, a connection, even in exile, to places on the earth. The students' anxiety thus probably came from the initial awareness of a non-connection and the realization of a dire need to start a process of connection in order to survive.

On the other hand, excitement seemed to come with the process and the attempts to make connection with place in spite of the difficulties that attended the attempts. Eniola described some of such attempts as trying "to order food and you don't even know what name to call it; you don't know what they call their own cabs." The seemingly contradictory experiences of difficulty and excitement seem to furnish additional avenues of learning for the student as they adapt to their new cultural environment. The difficulty of living in a specific place, with specific people, under specific conditions, many times, inspires reflection and a deeper understanding of what we really need in and for life. Place can teach us a healthy humility. That lesson is reflected in Eniola's statement that no one can be absolutely ready for living in a foreign place.

PEOPLE SLOWLY WARM UP TO YOU

Ruth was the first to describe the experience of being warmed up to. She described how, in her earlier months in the school, she would sit in the class and nobody would talk to her. She felt so alone, so lonely. She would go back to the dormitory only to experience the same thing. She said, "Nobody would say anything to me . . . people were so near, yet so distant. It was one of the worst feelings that one can have. It's terrible." "Whereas in Africa," Ruth explained, "When you come into a community, you find people are very open. They come to you, they ask you who you are and they take to you automatically so much so that, sometimes, there is even the danger of their invading your territory." Ruth concluded her story by saying, "When they eventually warmed up to me, it was a rewarding experience." It was rewarding because the experience signified acceptance and the beginning of a friendly and productive relationship. Ruth said, "We became friends, the best of friends. Now some of my best friends are from here (the U.S.)."

Eniola described a similar experience with particular reference to the classroom setting. She said: "Everyone comes in with their own suspicion and consciousness. It is like: 'I don't know how to relate to her; I don't know where she is coming from.'" She recollected that the first few days of class were lonelier and kind of dramatic, but as soon as people got to know her better, they 'warmed up' to her. People came closer and she made friends. She summarized the experience as that of, "Let's study her first and see who she is, and you study them first and see who they are, and you come together and become real good friends."

This experience would be significant to African students not only because it was rewarding but also because it made the students more aware of their African tendency to instantaneous warm up to strangers and visitors. Perhaps if the students knew of the initial distancing of others in advance, it would be a less stressful experience. An African student who was not prepared for an initial period of "checking out one another" thus experienced loneliness or even alienation while that period lasted. The loneliness that African and other foreign students experienced was therefore not only social in nature; it had significant cultural and interpersonal dimensions. The loneliness limited the students' initial interactions with other students. It was often related to the fact that African cultures emphasized kinship, family and communalism in sharp contrast to the American cultural values of independence, individualism and autonomy. What is it like for the students to make the transition between cultures with such a different emphasis? In what other ways was "being warmed up to" rewarding? How did the students reconcile their longing for communal cooperation with the demands for individualism characteristic of the society in which they were presently living?

FINDING INFORMATION

One of the earliest challenges African students had to struggle with was finding information that they needed to facilitate their experiences. As Abeke remarked, "There are a lot of opportunities in the U.S., I quite agree, but the problem is to get the information, to know whom to talk to, whom to ask, things like that." Sandra explained a similar difficulty saying: "The hardest part is the system whereby you have to find housing, to have installed telephones, class, lectures, and everything. Getting settled was difficult. Getting information about all those things was difficult."

It is partly understandable that the students, being strangers to the U.S., would need some time to adjust and settle down. Finding information about their needs during that period could be a source of hardship for them. There are, however, other things about the students themselves that made this aspect of their experience significant. The students seemed to have a different expectation regarding their initial contact with the school. Unlike many colleges in Africa where the students would be welcomed as a group, given bulletins of information about life on campus and assigned their rooms in the dormitories, the students very early discovered that they were very much on their own. This early introduction to self-independence seemed to cause some of the students some anxiety. Edna, for example, had this to say about the experience: "It still strikes me as odd that when you come to a school, you have to find yourself accommodation. You just have to find yourself everything. It is really different from Swaziland. It caused me some anxiety too."

Another source of difficulty regarding finding information by African students is the attitude of not asking. Sometimes this could be linked to language difficulty. There were some students who started out freely inquiring about what they needed to know but gradually stopped doing so for fear of being further ridiculed for their accent. Binu commented about this: "When you pronounce a word and someone laughs or giggles, it's very humiliating and demoralizing. I know of an African student not saying a sentence in class not because he doesn't know but because he doesn't want to be laughed at."

Knowledge is of two kinds; knowing something or knowing where to find information about it. How would students who do not know and who are too timid to ask, find needed information? Dayo's answer to this question was: "Students in general have to realize that it's not up to anyone else, it's up to you. If you don't find out for yourself, nobody is gonna do it for you. If you don't step out there and say, 'Hey, I need help,' nobody is gonna help. I've always found information; I always ask." Dayo was the only student who said finding information was not a problem for her. Her 'recipe' for finding information was to ask and to actively look for it.

FENDING FOR ONESELF

Being far away from parents and other family, students had to fend for themselves. This was a strange experience for Abeke. She recalled what it used to be like, going to school in Nigeria: "All you do is, go to school, that's it. Your parents or some elders in the family will be responsible for your expenses and things like that. You could go to other family members to ask for additional support. Whether or not you asked, some of them would give you the support anyway."

The student seemed to enjoy the dependence on family while going to school. The parents probably also enjoyed providing the support; it was the least they could do for a child who was aspiring toward what they profoundly valued, education.

Going to school and working at the same time, and fending for one's self caused the students a lot of stress. Sheila said, "It's rough and I'm just managing to cope." Abeke said, "It's kind of difficult . . . difficult to concentrate in class when you've worked like 12 hours the night before. Obviously you gonna fall asleep." What sustained the students in spite of the stress of the sudden call to self-reliance? What learning takes place for the student in this experience of fending for oneself? What transformation was unfolding as the students learned to fend for themselves?

BEING IN THE U.S IS AN OPPORTUNITY

Most African students considered their being in the United States as an opportunity. Even Abeke, who initially disliked coming to the U.S., later described the experience as "a great opportunity." Opportunity is the favorable combination of circumstances, time and place; it is a chance for advancement. What then are the circumstances that make coming to, or being in, the U.S. "a great opportunity" for African students? What is it about being in this place (America) that makes it an opportunity for the students? What does this time period of being in the U.S. offer African students? What is the nature of such offering?

Being in the U.S., for many African students, meant an opportunity for them to further their education. The students described various circumstances that led them to consider the experience as an opportunity. Dayo, for example, said that at a time when there were very few academic institutions and admission opportunities in Uganda, her fiancée invited her to join him in the U.S., a place that was offering abundant opportunity for schooling. It was a similar experience for Binu as he recalled his first impressions about the U.S., a place he described as "the citadel of knowledge particularly in terms of science and medicine."

Sandra's basis for describing being in the U.S. as an opportunity was slightly different. It was not related to the fact that institutions of higher learning were few in Malawi. Rather it was because the ones that were available did not offer the kind of program she wanted. She was looking for a master's degree program with a clinical nursing component. She applied to the United Kingdom and couldn't find any program that suited her purpose. Then she applied to the United States. She was happy to find many programs with the kind of clinical specialties she desired.

The circumstances surrounding Sandra's coming to the U.S. were similar to mine. One of the attractions that brought me to the U.S. was the potential opportunity to earn a doctoral degree in nursing. When I left Nigeria in 1991, none of the thirty universities in the country offered a Ph.D. program in nursing. In fact, only one was offering an M.S.N. program. So, for me, coming to the U.S. was indeed a double opportunity; on one hand, to better my economic status, on the other, to realize a dream of earning a Ph.D. degree in nursing. Being in the U.S. for many African students was therefore, being in a place where one could avail oneself to opportunities that were scarce or unavailable in one's home country.

Sometimes African students were selected and sponsored by their governments or by international organizations such as United States Agency for International Development (USAID) to come to the U.S. to continue their studies. People that were qualified or interested in applying for such programs usually far exceeded the number of scholarships being offered. So, those finally selected considered themselves as indeed fortunate and were exceedingly joyful. The joy was not limited to the fact that they got selected. It included the fact that the place where they would use the scholarship was no less a country than the United States of America! A place Binu described as "the citadel of knowledge." Ruth and Edna were lucky recipients of such scholarships.

Edna described how she was selected for a scholarship. Her country's Minister for Health was thinking of starting a nursing college and wanted people who had O' levels, which was equivalent to the twelfth grade in the U.S. She applied along with forty other people. She went through the screening, wrote several tests at the USAID office in Swaziland and was lucky to be among the six nurses who were selected.

Africans also consider themselves lucky to be studying in the U.S. when they contrast the variety and quality of educational opportunities available in the U.S. with those in their home countries. Fewer institutions of higher learning, unavailability of some graduate and other desirable programs, and poor teaching facilities characterize the educational systems of many African countries.

From the students' dialogue, the most important reason that brought Africans to the U.S. was education. The reason they choose to stay in the U.S. was the declining economies of their countries. This thus provides further insight into the context that made being in the U.S. an opportunity for many African students. Life dreams that they probably once thought were unrealizable in the unfavorable socio-economic circumstances of their home countries suddenly came within reach. The students, therefore, hold tenaciously to the newly available opportunity and, with all determination, tried to make the best of it. However, as they do so, one wonders, what are the challenging aspects of the opportunity? What makes it rewarding and exciting? What threatens the students' grasp of it? How do they sustain their grasp? What future do the students see as unfolding for them in taking the opportunity?

OPPORTUNITY TO LEARN FROM EXPERTS

African students described their experience as an opportunity to learn from experts. Ruth described this access to experts as "what I enjoy and value most as a student." She further explained that she enjoyed the exchange of ideas with the experts invited to workshops and seminars by the administration and student organization of her school in California.

An expert is someone whose knowledge or skill is specialized and profound, especially, as the result of much practical experience. Experts can stand the test of pressure from clients (e.g. students) as they call for answers to their questions, puzzles or needs. What is it like to learn from experts? What is it about experts that makes learning from them "one of the best experiences" for the students? Experts captivate their audience by the virtuosity of their knowledge and experience. They also captivate by skillfully guiding their students' collective thinking processes as they lead the expert-learner process. However, the African student's teacher must be especially aware of the double-edged sword nature of the authority image that comes with being seen as an expert. When someone is perceived as psychologically big, such as an expert, students expect that individual to solve problems, to see that all goes well, to take care of them, and to tell them what things to do and how. This dependence can lead to apathy and lack of initiative. Experts may present an image of a person who is competent, more intelligent and certainly more powerful. On the other hand they may be perceived as distant, controlling, dominating or even intimidating. This may cause students to feel less free and open in discussing or contributing their thoughts and ideas, particularly African students who already come with a mindset of awe even for the basic status of teacher. Teachers, therefore, need to be aware that being upgraded to the higher status of expert-teacher in the minds of their students could be both a source of admiration by some students and a cause of intimidation and alienation to others, especially African students, particularly during the earlier days of their experience in the U.S.

OPPORTUNITY TO PURSUE ONE'S DESIRED CAREER

African students described their being in the U.S. and securing admission into a school as an opportunity to pursue their desired careers. Abeke considered nursing "a good career because it was a highly respected profession in the U.S. whereas in Nigeria, doctors enjoyed far more social prestige than nurses." For Biola, nursing was a good career in the sense that it matched an interest for taking care of people that she had earlier developed as a young girl taking care of her 89-year old grandmother. Funmi similarly had an interest in nursing that far predated her admission to nursing school. She said she had "always wanted to be a nurse or be in something like a caring field, even though my parents wanted me to be an accountant." So, when she got to the U.S. she first proceeded to earn a degree in accounting, trying to first satisfy her parents' wish. She subsequently came back to nursing where her passion was. She remarked, "I did what they wanted, right? Now, I think I can go and do what will make me happy." Funmi's commitment to first satisfying her parents' wish demonstrated the African child's culturally rooted sense of reverence for the parents' wish.

Funmi seemed to find herself in-between her commitment to her parents' wish and her own interests and desire for nursing. The pull from personal interest and desire seemed so strong that she came back to nursing. In a similar manner, the caring interest embedded in Biola's past led her to choose nursing as a career and sustained her motivation through the program. She explained that she liked to be a nurse because she was a caring person. She said. "I'm happy that despite all the frustration I did not give up and I'm doing well in school. I know I'm pursuing something good, a good career that I will benefit from in the future. So I'm O.K. and am focusing on my studies."

African students thus saw their experience as an opportunity to pursue a career that has relevance to their present interest, one that has a strong connection to their past, and one that has usefulness to their future. I wonder what benefits the students see for themselves in nursing in the future. What other cultural and personal values embedded in the students' past translate into their present experience of the nursing career. What is it like to incorporate one's family and parental desires into one's career pursuit? What other desires provide the energy and motivation for the students as they grasp the opportunity of pursuing nursing as a career?

EXPECTATIONS AND DISAPPOINTMENTS

There were occasions that the students met with disappointments with regards to their expectations before they left home. Biola, for example, was disappointed to hear that she had to retake English and some other courses as prerequisites to nursing school. She said, "I was disappointed. What did they mean? To do all these courses again after going through a college degree in Africa . . . ?" Further into her experience, Biola met with another disappointment. She explained: "I thought because I've got a degree in Africa and one from Europe, when I got here I would be able to work. But it doesn't work that way. I felt disappointed."

The foregoing experiences regarding school admission and securing a job led the student to conclude that, life here is quite competitive. Biola could not imagine why someone with two degrees could not find a job. Following the disappointment and frustration, Biola started looking for other career opportunities. So, she took up the job of Nursing Assistant. She was also disappointed in various other ways: when, after completing her prerequisites to nursing school, she still "had to be on a waiting list for two years; when she "felt underestimated by other students" who derided her contribution in class and; when "other students did not even want to listen" as her group (all African) presented a class assignment. About the latter, experience, she said, "They didn't even have the patience of listening to us." Her disappointment and frustration were made lighter when "the instructor told the class that we did a good job."

Binu's experience of disappointment was related to faculty rather than fellow students. He said, "Some teachers recognize and respect some students more than other students in terms of contribution in class." This, he said, made him "feel disappointed because it means that students are not treated equally." He explained further: "It's like in the case of Animal Farm. All animals are equal but some more equal than the others. That is more or less the philosophy being practiced by some members of the faculty." This doesn't give students that are looked down upon the opportunity to learn in a very good atmosphere, he concluded.

Binu elaborated further that some faculty members seemed to think that anybody from Africa was stupid, that nothing good could come out of Africa. He observed that an African student might be making a good point but because of the fact that he was from Africa, had an accent, and did not dress or look like the others, his contribution was 'nonsense'. Then, another student, who was not an African, would make the same point and be praised by the teacher. Ruth described a similar experience regarding differential validation of students by a teacher. She said: "Sometimes people do not think that when you come from a certain part of the world, you know anything, you must be a 'tabula rasa'. Such people cannot accept your point until repeated by someone from their own circle. Then, it makes sense all of a sudden. You don't know how painful that kind of experience is until it happens to you."

I have had one of those experiences and I agree it was painful. In a particular class, I was the only male and one of the two African students in the classroom. A female white American professor taught the class. Any point I made in that class was either not acknowledged or barely acknowledged before the teacher moved on to the next student. That was not as painful as when another student repeated what I had just said, sometimes not as well as I thought I had, and the professor suddenly glowed with validation and admiration for the other student. I would be sitting there, thinking, "Wasn't that what I just said?" Sometimes I debated in my mind, why did she do that? She probably did not hear me. Or, maybe she did not hear me clearly. Was she getting back at me for having been tardy in the past? Or did my accent prevent her from hearing what I had just said? Or did I just get discriminated against?

The experiences described by students above are complex, especially in terms of identifying the root of their being derided, underestimated, shunned or unacknowledged. It was clear that the students were disappointed and frustrated. There were, however, a variety of possible reasons that could have accounted for the actions and reactions of the students and teachers involved. These included prior contacts or interactions between the persons involved. This is not to say that racial and other forms of discrimination were not a possibility. Indeed, they were. However, Binu's statement, for example, contained a number of personal assumptions. For example, it might be an assumption to say that a teacher ignores the student's point in class only because of the student's accent or mode of dressing. Nevertheless, the questions still arise, with an increasingly diverse student body, how is a teacher called to be? How can a teacher foster diversity and keep discrimination, or even the slightest resemblance of it, at bay?

African students therefore experience not only the sense of heightened visibility but also feeling of being invisible, excluded, and ignored by faculty and fellow students. They tended to be overlooked, given less time to respond to questions, interrupted more frequently, and not acknowledged or validated in the same ways as their European American counterparts. What is it like to be ignored, underestimated or unacknowledged in class? Was the students' sense of pride and self-esteem injured by stereotypes and invalidation? What ways can faculty best be prepared to understand diversity-related experiences in classroom and clinical settings?

ENCOUNTERING PREJUDICE

African students described occasional encounters, both within and outside the school, in which they considered people's attitudes and actions as based on race, color or accent. The students used different words to describe their experiences. This included bias, prejudice, being stereotyped, being underestimated and being discriminated against.

Bias is a temperamental or emotional leaning to one side. It is a natural word that is neither positive nor negative. When it becomes negative, however, it becomes a prejudice. Negative bias or prejudice is, therefore, an unfavorable, unjustified and unreasonable opinion or attitude. When one acts on prejudice, it becomes discrimination, and it is unfair. To discriminate against someone is to single out that person for unfavorable treatment. It is the making of unfair distinctions, in the treatment or service to others. To stereotype is to form a rigidly conventional expression or idea about a group of people or act towards someone from the group based on that idea. To be underestimated is to be rated below one's true worth. What is it like to be underestimated, stereotyped or discriminated against? How did the students experience those phenomena? What did the students learn from those experiences or encounters?

DIFFERENT WAYS OF SPEAKING

The students described their experiences with language, particularly their difficulty with accent. They realized that difference in accent made it difficult for them to understand and to be understood by others. Ben recalled, "Everyone was saying that I have an accent." Sheila said, "Sometimes I don't want to talk in class since they may not understand my accent anyway." Abeke described a more vivid example of this experience of how her accent made communication difficult for her. She said: "When you get up to talk, the instructor might not understand you. I would like to assume they are not doing that on purpose. But then, you can imagine if there is a whole hall full of, like 200 people and then I get up to ask a question and the instructor is looking at me like, 'what is she saying?' I mean that's embarrassing"

In the foregoing experiences, the students realized that the other person might truly have difficulty understanding their accents. Nonetheless, the experiences were embarrassing and painful to the student. The manner, countenance, attitude and handling of the situation by the teacher could make all the difference in the students' experience of those learning encounters.

Abeke described the most dramatic experience of how difficulty with her accent caused her tremendous frustration and threat to self-identity. She went to a drive-through restaurant and tried to order food. Twice she said, "Can I have one Number One and a coke please?" and twice the attendant replied, "I can't understand you." Finally, the attendant said, "I can't hear you ma'am, drive up to the window." So she drove up to the window and got out of the car. Then the attendant asked again, "What will you like to order?" Out of frustration, Abeke insulted her saying, "It's a number. It wasn't a long sentence, you know. So, how come you don't understand? What's there to understand? What is your problem? What don't you understand in 'one number one and one coke?' what do you need to understand?"

In this story the student was sure she spoke clearly understandable English but the attendant did not understand her even after several repetitions. The student became frustrated and upset. It was difficult for her to believe that the other person did not understand her because she thought her sentence was short, simple and clear enough. That the other person said she did not understand the student was like an assault to the student's self-identity. What do students learn when their accents get in the way of communication? What happens to learning when the student's self-identity is threatened? From Abeke's story, self encounters a crisis with its identity and felt urgently called to either reaffirm or re-invent itself. In that episode, it chose to reaffirm itself, but in a very emotional and rather verbally and attitudinally aggressive way.

Abeke described what she did when she could not understand others because of their accent. She said, "I just say yes even though I don't understand. I don't want to go through saying, "What did you say, I don't understand you." Someone might feel, 'Hey, she doesn't even understand English!' I'm very sensitive about the way people feel about me." For Abeke, showing that she had difficulty in understanding the other person's accent was like opening herself up for being branded as ignorant by peers or even the teacher. Rather than take that chance, she would pretend to understand the speaker when really she did not. Rather than have difficulty with the other's accent mistaken for difficulty with the subject matter, she would keep quiet to save herself from being embarrassed. Being a 'very sensitive' person, her dignity, self worth and self-esteem were more important to her. That however raises the serious pedagogical question of, what is it like for a student to feel perceived as ignorant? What do students learn when fear of being seen as ignorant keeps them from participating in learning? What happens to the quality of learning in situations of fear? Is Abeke's a case of one's voice being lost to the threat of self-identity? How can the students be encouraged to make their difficulty in learning known so they can be appropriately helped?

WHEN JUDGED BY ACCENT

Students told stories of difficulty with understanding and being understood by others sometimes that went beyond basic accent or language problems. Biola, for example said some of the other students "underestimate students from Africa especially because of our tonation." Funmi made a similar remark: "Because I sound this way some people think I'm stupid and I'm not. I always try hard to disprove them." The phenomenon of being underestimated carries with it the idea of worth. The experience might put students in a position to prove their self worth. Students might struggle to disprove others' rating of them that they perceived as below their true worth. What is it like to have one stereotyped and rated below one's perceived true worth? What happens to learning when its goal or context becomes the proving of self worth?

Stereotypes are mental categories based on exaggerated and inaccurate generalizations used to describe all members of a group. They are erroneous beliefs that multi cultural education aspires to eliminate. Prejudices and stereotypes speak to identity and difference. They derive from the meanings people make of self-identity and their difference from others. However, meaning is never immediately present in a sign. I, for example, do not begin the meaning of myself with myself but rather in relation with the others for whom I remain forever responsible. The meaning I make of the other determines whether I will be prejudiced or be open to care for the other when I meet the other face to face.

Dayo described her own experiences with being stereotyped as "subtle incidents." Once in her community college, she did a test in microbiology in which she did not do well. So she went to the instructor and asked, "Why wasn't this answer right?" and she said, "That's not the answer, you cannot expect me to be giving you people free points?" She said, "I was so upset I cried. I mean I worked hard. That was the summer I was taking three classes and was pregnant." In this episode Dayo was hurt because the teacher's reaction to her was based on a stereotype of a particular 'you people.' That was the same "you people" stereotype that incurred bitter confrontation for presidential candidate Ross Perrot from African Americans during the Presidential election campaigns of 1991. Dayo expected the teacher to address her as an individual rather than one of "you people," that, by implication, expected "free points" from the teacher.

In the following story told by Abeke, not being understood by the teacher was perceived and described as racial discrimination by the student. She was asking the instructor a question and the instructor said, "I can't hear you." She spoke louder and the instructor could not hear her still. The third time, the instructor said, "I can't understand you." One of Abeke's white American classmates repeated what Abeke had said and then the instructor understood. Abeke's reaction to that episode was, "Okay, the other student knew what I said but she couldn't understand me. How come? It's just basic simple English, you know. That's kind of frustrating and it's kind of upsetting. I mean — you feel embarrassed when something like that happens because you know there is a problem with race. That's why that's happening."

The student described this experience as "frustrating," "embarrassing," and "a problem with race." The student's experience and interpretation of this situation were thought provoking. It raised many fundamental phenomenological questions. The teacher had reacted differently to two students of different races and accents who were trying to make the same point. What does it mean to the African student to perceive being reacted to on the basis of race and on the basis of accent? How did the student come to assume that it was race and not difficulty with accent that underlined the teacher's behavior? Was the student's assumption based on the fact that she had repeated herself several times in order to make herself understood? Was it based on the fact that both she and the other student were speaking "just basic simple English"? What is "basic simple English?" What and how did this student's experience call the teacher to be? What will be the best culturally sensitive teacher response in this type of classroom situation?

LOSING AND FINDING ONE'S VOICE

African students' participation in class sometimes diminished, following certain experiences. Biola said she stopped asking questions in the class because teachers and classmates frequently remarked that they did not understand her. Sometimes, some of her colleagues even mocked her. She, therefore, resorted to reserving her comments or questions until after the class "to ask other African colleagues or go to the teacher." She discovered that was not a very effective way of learning for her. She believed she "would have gained a lot more from different opinions and discussions if they, (other students in the class) would only listen." For this student, voice was lost in the experience of being excluded and found in lived relation with others who listened. What is it like to lose one's voice in learning situations? What does a student learn without voice?

Ruth's participation in class discussion was very little when she first came to the school. This was because she did not understand the American accents and metaphors. She also found it difficult to follow the "Rapid pace and crisscross pattern" that characterized class seminars. She said learning was more difficult because "Americans used a lot of slang and colloquial English." This was an uncomfortable experience for Ruth. She said, "Before you know it the whole three hours of class are gone. And you wonder what you have been doing."

Voice came back for Ruth when she became so uncomfortable that she made a decision to always ask questions. What is it like for a student to be kept out of classroom discussion by a language barrier? The student's decision to speak up, to get back her voice was preceded by a period of being quiet. What happens to the self in that moment of quietness? Is that like the brief interval between the lightning and the thunder during which the self sleeps? Does the eventual roaring forth of the thunder then represent the emergence from silence of a new voice for the student?

Dayo had a stoic attitude toward the experience of losing voice. She issued forth a warning to other African students from her own experience: "You need not always be quiet when you have something to say." How true! Otherwise the student's voice might forever get lost in the "eternal silence that follows a thunderless lightning." Dayo explained that she not only found her own voice, she developed an assertive attitude with it. In fact, when she thought she was being ignored or brushed aside, she added assertiveness to voice.

ENCOUNTERING PLACES OF RACIAL DISCRIMINATION

Students also told stories about racial discrimination. Funmi's story was about the most dramatic. She once visited her sister and cousin in Independence, Missouri in the summer of 1995. She had taken her children to Chuckie Cheese. As soon as her son climbed into the Ball Basket, she said all the white kids came out and she was really embarrassed. She called the waitress and told her about what just happened and the waitress said "Yeah! They are racist in Independence." She remarked to herself, "All of them are kids, and they were already taught difference? I don't think I'll like to stay in this room." So, she took her son and left immediately. She said, "I never knew there were places where people were still treated in that way. I live in Baltimore and I've never encountered that. Gosh! I don't ever want to go back there. My sister said, "Yeah, this is Independence," and she laughed."

Ruminating about the experience later, Funmi said, "It wasn't like my son was as different or deformed as to have frightened those kids." She could not understand how children so young could be so much attuned to racial difference. This makes one wonder, are there accepting and non-accepting places? Do students learn differently in both places? What and how do students learn in non-accepting places?

Dayo observed that even in class, "You find the white students grouping together and the blacks, separately." Even though this type of segregation was mutual, it sent negative signals about place, self, and community and made most African students uncomfortable. The more a place values community, the more the African student feels welcomed. This probably explains why Funmi, in the Missouri experience, said "I took my kid and left the place immediately." In addition to students grouping together on the basis of color, Dayo remarked, "African Americans also sometimes stereotype and discriminate against Africans. They say we behave as if we are cleverer than them and some of them feel we have come to deprive them of their economic opportunities."

No matter the cause of prejudice or discrimination, the one being discriminated against is usually left with some feeling of negative self-image. What negative self-image did Africans get from prejudice and discrimination? Do African Americans really see African immigrants as usurping their positions, depriving them of opportunities or causing them undesirable social change? What is it like for a stranger to be seen as a usurper or an agent of unwanted change?

CONSIDERING CHANGING MY NAME

Abeke remarked that, "There have been times when I have thought of changing my name to an American name so that when it appears on paper, it does not have to be a problem." This was perhaps one way by which some Africans attempt to protect themselves from discrimination. It is a way of protecting one's self by forgoing one's name, a strong component of self identify. Considering the tremendous sacredness and importance that Africans attach to names, it could, indeed, be a very painful way of self-protection to voluntarily shed one's name. This sacredness, on the other hand, explains why some Africans would not consider changing their names, no matter how much their names caused them discrimination.

Prejudice is an integral part of human nature. Everyone, including the African student, is, in one way or the other, biased. Our biases are not only pre-existing lenses for understanding ongoing experiences, they are also part of our being. They determine our regard of, presence with, and relationship to others. They are, in a sense, our pre-understandings of life and its situations. Through biases we come to identify ourselves as different and apart from others. The students' stories underscored the fact that prejudices hurt when they are unfounded. Also, whether justified or unfounded, prejudices hurt if they are considered the basis of an unfair treatment. The readiness to lose one's name, an asset that most Africans treasure, in order to protect one's self from social and emotional pain, was a good index of the intensity of that pain. What is it like for an African who attaches so much meaning to name to abandon name for self-protection? How are name and self-identity related to learning?

African students narrated stories of encounters with unfamiliar ways of being. These included ways of speaking, norms about touching, and meanings of respect that were different from what the students were familiar with in Africa.

UNFAMILIAR METAPHORS

Students' stories regarding language were related not only to difficulty with accent but also, with American metaphorical expressions. Ruth said, "You can go to a class and spend three hours and not know what they are talking about because they may use so many metaphors." She explained how she got around that difficulty: "So, I decided I was not going to be keeping quiet. Anytime someone used any metaphor I don't know, I asked them to explain it and they did."

This experience of not being understood led Ruth to redirect attention to her self and rediscover herself in relation to language while in a different place. It was understandable how a conversation or class discussion would be difficult for Ruth. She did not have a prior shared understanding of the metaphors being used and of the culture from which the metaphors originated. Sheila's feeling of intimidation to talk in class for fear of her accent being mocked, Abeke's frustration and embarrassment with accent, Funmi's and Biola's feelings of being underestimated, all portrayed an intricate relationship between place, language and self.

Language is loaded with meaning rooted in the culture of a particular place. Lack of familiarity with a place or with the culture, therefore, creates difficulty with language and, in turn, anxiety for the self. Granted, that difficulty with accents and metaphors lead to frustration, embarrassment and feeling of inadequacy, where do the students go from here? What do students learn when the language skills of which they have been hitherto proud become ineffective in a different place?

Ruth's approach to surmounting her language difficulty seemed more pedagogically productive. She said she decided she "was not going to keep quiet." Whenever anyone used a metaphor she did not understand, she "asked them to explain it and they did." By developing a positive attitude, an attitude of genuine interest to understand language, including its metaphors and cultural roots, Ruth started to forge human and cultural connections between her and others. She started to change from being a stranger to being well grounded and connected to others in her new abode. What new selves are emerging for African students in relation to learning new ways of speaking?

TO TOUCH OR NOT TO TOUCH?

Two students narrated experiences in which they were instructed not to touch the patient during their clinical nursing orientations. Ruth recalled an episode that happened the third day she took a clinical nurse job in a critical care unit. The manager came and told her that they did not want her to touch the patients. "That was a shock to me," she said. She was a registered nurse. Yet, there were nursing assistants there touching the patients. She further remarked, "How could I take care of patients without touching them? I found that insulting and infuriating . . . as if they did not think I knew anything about patient care. That was a humiliating experience. That was one of my worst experiences." She requested a change of units and found the staff of the new unit "very open-minded." She enjoyed working there. What would make a manager instruct a newly employed nurse not to touch the patients? Had any student touched a patient in an improper manner prior to this episode and the nurse manager did not want that incident to be repeated? Had the manager experienced a similar episode with African students that called for this type of caution or restriction? Had the patient requested that restriction from the unit authority? What do students learn under such 'non-touch' restriction? What is it like to be under such restrictive instruction? What does the student need to question in this situation?

Binu narrated a similar experience but with a different interpretation. "I was given a patient to care for but the nurse in charge wouldn't allow me to touch the patient, wouldn't even allow me to do anything for the patient. That made me say, 'I would like to be treated as a human being'." Asked for further details about this experience, Binu said the charge nurse who disallowed him from touching the patient later explained to him that she had been upset before she got to work that day and that her action was just a transference reaction. Reacting to that, Binu said, "I don't believe that excuse, it's simply discrimination." If he was right, what does a student learn in such a discriminating clinical setting? If not, what other undisclosed reasons might precipitate the nurse's action? What was it about the nurse, the student, the patient or the context that could have given rise to this episode?

As fate would have it, I was visiting a hospital about two months after this conversation and was talking with a clinical instructor. Aware that I am an African, the instructor shared with me how one of her students, an African male, put his hand on a female patient's leg as a way of showing support. She said this behavior disturbed everyone present, including the unit nurses and the student's peers. As the instructor was narrating this story, the student walked by and it turned out to be Binu. Even though this student's interpretation of the incident was racial discrimination, this last development suggested the possibility that some of his actions might reflect different cultural practices related to touching. There are differences in manners and frequencies of touching within the American context compared to an African context. In most African cultures, touching each other during conversation is generally freer. Holding each other's hands while walking on the street (irrespective of gender) would be commonplace in an African society. On the other hand, kissing and hugging may be less frequent. To what cultural sensitivity issues do African students need to be attuned, especially prior to clinical exposure?

A DIFFERENT MEANING OF RESPECT

The African students believed that American students did not "respect" their teachers enough. At least, not as much as you would find in an African school context. Biola remarked about this issue. She said back home in Africa, students gave a lot of respect to their teachers. The students here seemed to lack that type of respect. She said, "I know there's academic freedom, but back home, you still respect your teachers. You let them talk. You don't talk back, you don't growl or murmur when they are talking. That is disrespect. Anybody who is your teacher, you don't look them in the eyes."

Respect is directly related to various forms of social hierarchies within the African cultural context, the most prominent ones being age and social status. It is demonstrated by conspicuous obeisance, for example, by a younger person to an older person or by a student to a teacher. It can be so profound that, to argue with your teachers, interrupt when they are talking or call them by their first names would be deemed discourteous or even downright disrespectful. Coming from such a background to an educational setting with a more egalitarian teacher-student relationship, the African student, at worst, might receive a culture shock and at best, might quickly realize that she had a good deal of cultural adjusting to make.

The African students soon discovered that student behaviors that depicted respect in Africa were different for the American context. Examples of such behaviors, from the students' experience, were: not looking the one to be respected in the eyes; not engaging in side talk while the teacher was talking; and not interrupting the teacher. To look the teacher in the face in the American culture might be an indication of being attentive. To the African student it was disrespectful. To interrupt a teacher and ask a question might be considered creditable within the American context, for at least trying. In fact if you did not try, you might have failed; the trying or the attempt itself counted for something—it was often considered as important as the actual activity. To the African students, such interruptions were disrespectful. Many professors granted that students call them by their first names. Some students even did so, irrespective of the teacher's consent. In the African context, that would be equally disrespectful. It would take an African student some time, effort and courage to start doing that. For me it did. I had to constantly remind myself that, "When you are in Rome, you do as Romans" before I could bring myself to addressing any of my professors by their first names. This, often times, is easier said than done. What is it like for African students to adjust to the differences in the meanings of respect and other relational behaviors?

IT'S LIKE BEGINNING ALL OVER AGAIN.

In order to be admitted to nursing school, the African students, including those who were already registered nurses from their respective countries, needed to take about sixty credits of prerequisite courses including English. Biola said the experience "was like starting from the beginning again; it was frustrating." Similarly Eniola remarked, "I was a nurse in Nigeria. I came here and passed the Registered Nurse (RN) board exam on the first sitting. Yet, they were not going to give me any credit for any of the courses I had taken. They gave me a list of prerequisites like 84 credits in order to go in for a 33-credit program! It's frustrating."

Ben also described the experience as "like starting all over again." Biola gave a sequential narration of the frustration and disappointment she experienced with the admission process. Her frustration was due to her being on a nursing school admission waiting list for more than two years. The students' disappointment and frustration derived from their expectation that their previous educational qualifications would translate to American requirements, course for course and credit for credit. They probably also expected an easier admission to school than they experienced. Then, they discovered that they needed to retake some of their courses. What is it like to use precious time to do all over again something you think you have done and completed? Eniola described the experience as frustrating. Many students proceeded to take the prerequisite credits anyway since they were resolved to take nursing and they saw no other alternatives.

FIRST YEAR WAS LIKE THUNDERSTORM

The first year was very crucial for the students because they were not only going through the stress of schoolwork; they were adjusting to a different environment and culture. Abeke described her experience of the first year, saying, "The first year in nursing school was like thunderstorm. It was going so fast that I couldn't figure out what was going on until the end of the first semester. I was very confused. It was just very frustrating. It wasn't too good."

Other students described what made this early part of their experience so confusing and stressful. Eniola said, "The first few days were the loneliest and they were kind of dramatic." She later added: "It took me far into the first semester to realize that the textbook sometimes doesn't really count as much as what the lecturer says. . . . Now I read for the points that are important to the course." Eniola spoke about how her approach and perspective of school needed to quickly change if she was to survive the "thunderstorm." One important thing she needed to change was her reading style. The student realized that there was such a broad spectrum of details to master that there was no time to waste, dwelling on every detail provided in textbooks.

Ruth further contrasted the emphasis in education between America and South Africa. She said, "Our educational system is very focused, very deep and detail-oriented. . . . Here, the educational system is very broad. In a semester, they peg so much in. They are not so much concerned with the details but the application of the content to everyday life or to some specific area." Ruth explained how this contrast constituted a source of stress. She said, "Being used to a system where you had one year to master what we now learn in one semester, is a stressful situation. All of a sudden, you have to cram in all that information in one semester. Before you know it, it is the semester exam. That is very stressful to my brain."

Funmi said she was "lost and drowning." She said, "The schoolwork was just too much, especially the first semester. Without having any experience of what I was doing, it was just too much." Dayo recalled a discovery that she made in the experience. "I discovered that I needed a lot of patience because everything seemed to be coming down on me. Everything seemed to be demanding to be done in a different way. That's when a couple of African friends dropped out of the program."

It was not only that there were significant differences between the pace and emphasis of education as the students experienced it in Africa and in America, there was also a difference in the expectation for student independent learning. Sandra, talking about what she would advise African students to know prior to coming to the U.S., said, "First, they would have to be made aware that the educational system is totally different from the educational system in Africa. Here, you're on your own for most of the time. There is no babysitting of students in this place." Perhaps if African students had prior knowledge of the breadth, briskness, and independence that characterized American education as contrasted with the African, the students' experience of the first semester or year would have been less "like a thunderstorm."

The metaphor of thunderstorm can be understood more deeply if approached from the standpoint of an African. For one thing, a thunderstorm is a climate condition that a Nigerian, such as Abeke, would understand in a particular sense. She might not be too familiar with snowstorms, earthquakes, hurricanes, blizzards, or tornadoes. But thunderstorms, she would understand them in their catastrophic proportions. It is thus understandable how the metaphor of "thunderstorm" would readily resonate with Abeke, offering itself as a means of making more sense of the criticality of her first year in an American college.

Secondly, thunderstorms were not usually predicted. There were no sophisticated means to forecast weather in most African countries as there were in the U.S. Thunderstorms struck suddenly. If reaching disastrous proportions, they might tear down trees and houses, blowing away people's valuables and sending people, pets and livestock into a frantic frenzy. They were usually a combination of heavy rains, thunder, lightening, winds and flooding.

Thirdly, there were post-thunderstorm stories of people who had been struck by thunderbolts in very heavy thunderstorms. Underlying these stories was the belief that 'Sango,' the god of thunder, sometimes struck people with thunderbolts for stealing from their neighbors. Some Yorubas even believed that you or your property could be a victim of stray thunderbolts. Severe thunderstorms could therefore be a time of extreme panic, confusion and anxiety. People running for survival, frantically protecting what was valuable to them from being blown or swept away, and hoping that they would not be struck by a lightening bolt! When the storm abated, anxiety settled and visibility became clearer. One breathed a sigh of relief, thanked God for surviving, and pulled oneself together to continue with life that seemed to have been temporarily put on hold in the moment of that confusion. What did the African student learn through the "thunderstorm" experience? What promoted growth and survival in the "thunderstorm" experience? What prevented the fatal trauma of a "lightening bolt?" What transformation occurred at the end of "the storm?" What could enhance that transformation?

The experience brought students closer to talk and work together. Just like survivors of thunderstorms and other natural disasters, they identified with a common past experience and a common future course, that of healing and forging ahead. The student drew strength in the dawning awareness that, though the thunderstorm was individually experienced, it was not self-caused. The student could now see other people that were in the storm that she was too confused to see while the storm was blaring and blazing. The 'confusion' and 'frustration' seemed to relate to the suddenness and the unexpected nature of the storm. The students thus appeared to have been jolted into panic and hyper vigilance characteristic of storm victims rather than into readiness and alertness that a weather forecast could have provided. Perhaps, a prediction of the possible storminess of the first year could have been helpful in making the 'jolt' less confusing. This probably could have been achieved by arranging for new and more senior African students to meet and share stories around what could be new and strange in the experience that was immediately ahead of the incoming students.

Through the thunderstorm experience Eniola modified her reading style and Dayo discovered her need and capacity for patience. Does the "thunderstorm" experience then have some growth-promoting potential? At what point does stress and confusion stop being growth-promoting in learning and become devastating and crises-laden? What support could teachers provide African students experiencing the "thunderstorm" phenomenon?

LEARNING TO SURVIVE OBJECTIVE TESTING

The students expressed difficulty with the objective mode of being tested. This method was strange to most African students who were more familiar with the essay type of student evaluation. Describing her difficulty with the objective tests, Abeke employed various metaphors to drive her point home. She said, "It's kind of tough because the way we are being tested is very different. I'm used to essay type of questions where you can write as much as you can but the objective is like do or die. You either get it or you don't. . . . The answers are closed. It's black or white, no gray."

Biola said she was used to the essay type of test in which she could "discuss the issue overall." Eniola remarked, "I come from a place where you have to know everything like inside out and explain it, but here it's like it's either a or b or c or d." Funmi said the objective test was a handicap to her. She asked. "How could you express yourself with only one right answer?" And she concluded, "That's why I cannot do my best on those exams. If I had my way, I will request they make the exam one half objectives and one half essays." Dayo was the most articulate in her opinion about the objective test. She said, "I want to get the chance to tell you what I know about the subject. Don't give me four choices. I can't do that. . . . When you see A, B, C, D, E, you are like, 'Good heavens! All those things apply! If you'll just give me a chance to tell you how they apply, I will even do that faster!"

It took some practice for the students to adjust to the objective testing. The essay type of exam that they were used to, usually called for description, explanation and sometimes, discussion. Whereas the objective tests they now had to confront often required making fine judgments between almost equally plausible options. The students therefore needed to transition from one mindset to the other in order to feel comfortable with objective testing. What is it like for the students to make this transition? What facilitates the transition? What impedes it?

THE COMPUTER IS A BIG THING

Except for Dayo who had learned to type and use the computer while attending the American University in Kenya before coming to the U.S., all the other students experienced difficulty with using the computer. She explained that many of the Africans who come to the U.S. have never touched a computer. Even though there were many such resources that could help the students to learn to use the computer, the students were sometimes intimidated.

48   *Chapter Four*

The students could not always find peers to help them through problems encountered in the process of using the computer because such peers also had their own assignments to do. However, the inability to get the attention and help of peers was interpreted differently by different students in different contexts. For example, Biola recalled that when she had some computer related assignments and asked some classmates for help in the computer lab and got a negative response, she felt disappointed. She did not feel free to ask them for help the next time because, she said, "I don't want them to shun me off again."

The computer and the other forms of educational technology are obviously meant to facilitate teaching and learning. For many African students, however, the computer represented a difficult means for learning, at least initially. Its use for various class assignments was one of the skills the African students needed to quickly learn at the beginning of their experience otherwise it got in the way. In what ways did the difficulty with using the computer inhibit the students' drive and passion for learning?

African students not only overcame most of the challenges they encountered, they also did well in their academic pursuits. Dayo, for example, said "I had to juggle all those roles, one way or the other, and come out successful. . . . I came out on top." What helped the students to keep up in spite of hardships? What facilitated their persistence and success? What is it like to succeed in a strange place and "come out on top?" Abeke said: "I have been going to school every semester, never failed a class and never repeated a class. So, I feel good about myself." What is it like to feel good about oneself? What helped the students to keep up until the experience of feeling good about oneself unfolded? These questions are further explored in the following sections.

GREAT VALUE FOR EDUCATION

African students portrayed an attitude that being educated was of primary importance in their lives. To them it was unimaginable not to have education as one of one's life priorities. These attitude and belief in education seemed to be intimately tied to most Africans' values and what their parents said or did about education. Abeke explained, "In Africa, you just have to get your education. That's part of my motivation. . . . I'm not a straight 'A' student. I'm an average student and I like to study. What else will I be doing if I'm not studying?" Once again, this student re-echoed the African value for education. It was a value that was culturally transmitted and so strong that it provided motivation for many African students. It was based on the belief that education represented the single most powerful factor for breaking socio-economical barriers. It probably also explained the severity of the feeling of devastation expressed by African students when they experienced academic failure. For some of the students, it was as if their life hopes were all coming, crumbling down.

Abeke recalled the roles of her parents in her motivation for learning. She said, "My dad always brings out his degree certificates and shows them to us on the first day of every year. He's so proud of them. I like to obtain my degree so that I can show it to my kids too. That's something to be proud of. . . . My mom also tells us to get a degree so we won't end up getting a job we'd be sorry for." Both parents, in different ways, impressed the value of education on their daughter's mind. Abeke retold her mother's story with passion. She actually sang one of her mother's songs of encouragement that happened to be one that my mother also sang. So I found myself joining the student in the singing during our conversation. Such literary and family-based experiences continued to live with students and seemed to provide them with inspiration from time to time. The African students' value for education provided some insight into how the students could have seen their being in the U.S. as a great opportunity. It provided, in part, the motivation and determination that the participants showed in the pursuits of their studies and career.

STRONG DETERMINATION TO SUCCEED

African students demonstrate great determination to succeed in spite of the obstacles and challenges they encounter along the way. This influences the way they relate to their peers, teachers and to significant moments of their experiences. When students tend to be frustrated they remind themselves of the efforts they have so far invested in the program and what lies ahead to be gained. Convincing themselves that they cannot afford to waste past investment, and that the imminent degree means a lot to their lives and to their extended families, they renew their drive to proceed and their determination to succeed.

FOR BETTER, FOR WORSE

All the students were determined to complete their course. For example, Eniola said, "Once you decide to take it, you take it with the good and the bad of it." However, Abeke expressed by far the most inflexible commitment to her program. She said, "It's stressful going to school and working. I don't have a choice. I have to cope. I have to work. It's like a marriage. It's for better for worse. I'm determined to get to where I am going, no matter what, regardless of the obstacles."

The metaphor of marriage used by Abeke is laden with deep cultural meaning. Marriage, within the African context, is a very enduring bond. It involves a very strong commitment not only from the two primary individuals but also from their families and extended families. This was probably why the student chose it as the metaphor to depict her commitment to her educational program. The involvement and seriousness of the two bride's and groom's families in marriage strengthened the bond and made it quite unthinkable for either the wife or husband to even contemplate divorce. What called for this type of commitment? The student had invested a lot in coming to the U.S. They had worked so hard to secure the many credits required for getting admitted into the program and, to progress thus far in it.

There were other things that underlined the African students' determination to succeed. They strove not to disappoint friends and relatives back home in Africa who had high hopes and admiration for them for being in the U.S. and for being on their way to earning a degree. A lot of extended family responsibility rests on most African students. They were aware that they were not in the U.S. for themselves alone. They had many dependents back in their home countries that were looking up to them for support, especially, financial. To fail in one's chosen career was therefore to disappoint not only oneself but also others looking up to one. Attempts to avoid this double jeopardy contributed to the strong determination by African students to succeed.

Dayo told several personal stories and used many metaphors to explain that the African student was ready to endure whatever it takes to get through school. She described enduring as "Filling the potholes on the road to success." To fill the potholes was to make the journey smooth. She recalled that when she came to the U.S., her daughter was six months old. Her daughter had since learned that they had bills to pay, they had things to be done, and you did not always get what you wanted. It was O.K. to drink water if there was no soda. She recalled her daughter saying, "Okay mom, I know you don't have money but can we just walk through the toy store?" And they did that so many times; they walked through the toy store, just so the daughter could look at toys. This story exemplifies one way that the student used to "fill the potholes" of economic constraint and pressing family needs. In this story, walking through the toy store afforded the child a chance to at least look at, probably sometimes play with, the toys that her mother was too poor to buy for her.

Dayo also "filled the potholes" with regard to lack of textbooks, using a combination of supports from friends, the library and her own determination.

She said, "Very few people know this; I finished nursing school with two or three textbooks. For the entire first semester, I had no books. I saw what people were using in class and I went to the library to read it and I never failed a single course. So, if you are determined to do a thing, you can do it. It's endurance. It's determination."

African students demonstrated a very strong determination to succeed. However because many had financial responsibilities for themselves and for their extended families and friends back in their home countries, they had to manage through school. For example, Dayo's claim that she could only buy two or three books throughout the entire B.S. program was not uncommon among the African students. As a result they depended, in the main, on the library facilities and exchange books among their circles of friends. Furthermore, most African students detested taking loans because of their cultural stigma about debts. Some of them, however, received scholarships.

BEING FOCUSED

African students channeled their energy and determination into not allowing the challenges of being a stranger distract them from achieving their respective goals. This tenacity shows in the following remarks by Eniola. "Since here nobody understands where you came from, you have to understand where you are going and abide by the rules. It could get really stressful. But I had my focus I had my plans and I am going to get it. As the saying goes, you take what you want in life, pay for it and move on. That's what I'm doing, moving on." In spite of challenges and difficulties, Eniola was resolved nothing would distract her from her focus. In order to do that successfully she seemed to believe that one must be ready to pay the price demanded of a stranger to a new place. Part of the price was to know the values, requirements and standards of the place and to "abide by the rules" that opened doors to success.

The students recognized that keeping focused called for the capacity to endure, the need to pay the price of being a stranger and the readiness to abide by the rules of one's new place of being. What is missing in the students' lives when their attention has been directed and concentrated on a single goal, that of earning a degree? From my personal experience, many other important aspects of one's life suffer. In the five years that I was in the doctoral program, I had a vacation once. When school closed, I increased my work hours in order to pay accumulated bills and still have some money left to send to my family, parents and extended families back in Africa.

Taking care of extended families by African students was culturally a matter of course. It called for no questioning. When school reopened, all my focus was back on completing schoolwork. It was like all other aspects of my life were put on hold for the sake of school. Such persistence, endurance and hardiness are referred to, in Nigerian parlance, as being rugged. What was the root of such ruggedness as seen in African students? Of what usefulness are the African students' hardiness to the students' learning and their being in the U.S.? What does hardiness have to do with being a student?

MAKING SACRIFICES

Students believed that they had invested a lot and made considerable sacrifices by immigrating, living and studying in the U.S. and they were determined to endure until it paid off. It was a sacrifice to leave behind the familiarity, security and comfort of home. The intimacy and company of loved ones were also experiences they had to forgo in order to be in the U.S. Even while here, there were many life adjustments they had to make in order to pursue their career. Funmi referred to the investment as a sacrifice. She recalled: "It was just much work. I don't know how I coped. I just try to do everything. I wasn't going to give up because I had sacrificed a lot, including my job with an accounting firm. I gave up my kids, taking them to the day care. Even my husband, we barely saw each other."

Similarly, Biola described the sacrifices she has had to make. Many times she felt frustrated in the process but proudly noted that, "Despite all the frustration, I did not give up." Dayo also recounted, "All our savings were gone. I had given all my paycheck to the babysitter. . . . It was challenging. Sometimes I find I am focusing so much on the schoolwork. I may not even be able to prepare a decent meal for my kids and my husband. . . . I feel it's a sacrifice and it's better to do it now." Abeke recalled moments of discouragement when she had to remind herself she had to "trade off" endurance for the gain that laid ahead, the degree. It was then that all her sacrifice could eventually "pay off." She said, "If you start to look at the things that are in your way such as the communication problems and the like, you will start to get depressed but if you think of the bright side, it's a good trade off. If I think of what I have been through, I would say, it has to pay off somehow. It just has to. So, I keep going."

The foregoing remarks exemplified how the students had invested in their careers and how much they expected an equivalent reward. African students have the attitude that, in the United States, all things being equal, one was usually assured of a positive reward for one's hard work. That may not necessarily be true of many African countries today. The prevailing sociopolitical circumstances in many African nations make it difficult to realize equivalent rewards for one's hard work. Thus, for the African students in the U.S., though the road to success might be laden with difficulties and challenges, the tacit and implicit assurance or at least hope, of a happy ending was gratifying and sustaining. It was worth making the sacrifice.

Sacrifice is the act of depriving oneself of something for the sake of attaining something else. The African students were very much familiar with the idea of sacrifice. It was something traditional healers in Africa frequently prescribed for people seeking such good things of life as health, prosperity, fortune, spouse, good luck, children and protection from evil machinations. The traditional healer was the one who specified the sacrifice, usually something of considerable value to the client. By using the sacrifice metaphor, the student, therefore, signified how valuable both the degree and the investments she had made in it were to her. What happens to learning when the sacrifice does not pay off as in the case of academic failure? What happens to the student's sense of pride and self-esteem in such circumstances? In the African context, when people failed to realize what they had sacrificed for, the healer usually offered an insight to explain away the sacrificial failure. Reasons were usually closely related to various aspects of the patient's being. In spite of the earlier failure, a bonding, based on a mutually shared, cultural, magical and mythical belief system, usually sustained trust and respect between client and healer as they planned another sacrifice. What does the teacher do when the African student experiences academic failure? What ways can teachers and students bond while learning takes place? What is the best way for teacher and student to proceed with planning "another sacrifice" when one has failed?

ACCOMMODATING INSTRUCTORS

Binu, the same student who narrated stories of the bitter experiences he had with some teachers, said many faculty members were good to him. He said, "Some faculty members are really good . . . very accommodating. They give encouragement. They know me by name. They call me by name and they say "hi!" and give me words of encouragement and words of wisdom, and I really like that. It gives me a lot of vim and vigor to go on." Similarly, Abeke recalled, "I have met a lot of people, including teachers in this school who were nice, you know, very kind and accommodating."

The student's idea of a good teacher included being accommodating. The word accommodating derives from the Latin word, "accommodare," which means "to adapt oneself to the other's convenience". In other word, it means to rearrange one's own affair for the other to be, and be convenient. Teachers who were accommodating, who gave words of encouragement, who recognized the person of the student and, who were caring were seen as good teachers. They transmitted energy to the student to move on, to grow, to become. What does it take to be an accommodating teacher? What else, besides being accommodating makes a good teacher for the African student?

FRIENDS' SUPPORT

Dayo narrated vivid experiences that led her to conclude that, "You are always going to have friends around you who understand, people who want to help." Many times all that was necessary was to ask. She said, "I had people around me who bought every single book that we needed. What was left for me to say was, 'Hey, this is my situation. If you are not using that book, do you mind lending it to me?'" At the end of the semester she had people bringing her books they had saved for her and a lot of them were Americans. She said, "They even took notes for me because sometimes, I went to class very tired, and they already saw it in my eyes that I was tired." What happens to learning when we foster caring and community in education?

FAMILY SUPPORT

Students who lived with their spouses or families described them as very supportive as they went through their school experience. Abeke explained that her husband was very supportive of her in everything. She said, "He helps me out with aspects of my schoolwork that I don't understand since he has a degree in science. Also, I can get home and talk to him. That makes me feel a little bit better, you know, in getting things off my mind and talking things out."

The idea of having someone to talk with and getting things off one's mind seemed to be a great relief for students who had their families with them. Abeke said the experience would have been "more stressful and frustrating if everyday, I would have to go home to be by myself and think about everything that happened during the day." Biola also described the encouragement she got from her family. "My kids, anytime I come home, they'd say, "Mommy how is school today?" And my husband, he will always say, 'you have to keep on, no matter how difficult. Just believe everything will be O.K' He also works and supports me financially, although I too work sometimes."

Biola's experience showed how the family's caring through emotional, financial and spiritual support kept her going. Particularly in times of stress or crisis, the family's role in sustaining the student was immense. For example,

Funmi said, "It was my husband who rescued me from drowning," referring to her overwhelming first semester experience. She said she considered herself "lucky to have a husband as supportive as he is." Living with one's family or spouse provides considerable support. It had its stressful aspects too. Dayo described how stressful it was for her to "juggle the roles" of student with those of mother and wife. She said it was "the greatest part" of her challenge.

HAVING FAITH IN GOD

Spirituality was an integral part of most African students' lives. Many of the students referred to God and how He had been their main source of support as they sojourned in the U.S. Dayo said, "God gives me life in spite of my needs and wants." Biola recalled her husband's constant reminder to her to always pray.

Most African students had grown up in families that practiced some form of religion. The students thus made constant inward recourses to these deep-seated spiritual beliefs as part of their inner strength. Apart from the fact that religion is an essential and integral part of many of the students' lives, apprehension about violent crimes and absence of family and extended family further reinforced the students' religious tenacity. Dayo's husband's injunction, "pray before you go out," was, to a great extent, a reminder to his wife to invoke an inner spiritual power against the perils "outside." Also, since the students' families, the greatest support systems they enjoyed while in Africa, were here absent, spirituality needed to be enlivened.

NOT CONSULTING WITH FACULTY

If there was one single benefit of the American educational system that African students did not take full advantage of, it was the opportunity for students to relate closely and to consult with faculty on a one-to-one basis. Abeke confessed: "Although, to be sincere, the instructors create time for students to come and consult them but I am not used to that kind of system, where you go to the instructor one-on-one and things like that." Biola had a similar attitude. She said, "I don't have much relationship with the instructors. I just believe that when I'm doing well in my courses, I don't need to go to any faculty member."

The attitude of "not going to faculty" was prevalent among African students even when students had problems. Even at times when consultation with faculty could have benefited the students' schoolwork, they still tended to keep a distance from their teachers. This was probably due to the idea that the students had brought with them with regards to student-teacher relationship. However, it is important to note here that in Africa today, school climate is gradually changing from that of absolute teacher power and control to a more collaborative student-teacher relationship.

In order for faculty and students who experience this phenomenon to come to a common understanding of the students' difficulties and needs, faculty will need to initiate dialogues and consultation most of the time. What, in stead, provided the guidance and resourcefulness that consultation with faculty would have afforded the African students? What did faculty members make of the distance created by this phenomenon of students' non-consultation with faculty?

HIDING A SORE FINGER

Apart from not consulting with faculty, some African students did not seek help from other people even when the help was really needed. This phenomenon might be due to the students' uncertainty about how and where to seek particular help. In some cases it was very closely linked to the acute sense of shame that the African tended to attach to failure, as earlier discussed. Not seeking help would become very crucial, with a student who has experienced failure. It was important for faculty to be aware of the cultural consideration that, often, African students might not seek help even when they actually needed it. Then, the faculty would be able to take the initiative for opening dialogue for a productive working together.

NOW AND THE FUTURE

African students had a vision of what could possibly make the experience easier and more gainful for them and future African students. This included being mentored by more senior African students, having activities that brought various cultural groups together more frequently, and continuous update of teachers on issues of cultural diversity and cultural sensitivity.

Funmi expressed the opinion that an organized system where new students were paired with more experienced students from similar cultures would be helpful to future students. She said, "At least the older students can constantly remind the new ones to stay focused and don't let anything bother them, don't let anything get to them because there is always going to be a lot of things that will get to them." This is like the weather forecast function. In Funmi's opinion, constant words of encouragement and forewarning by someone who had "been there" would give the new students a sense of what lie ahead and help them re-channel their energies toward the important directions.

Abeke expressed a similar view to that of Funmi. She said that one of the things that could have been helpful was to have something like a mentor program for people who had been through the program, who had done well and have graduated to share their experience. She said, "When you are feeling confused and frustrated and lost, you find someone that can tell you, 'I've been there before and here I am today.'"

In this comment, Abeke revealed that the experience of being reassured might be an integral part of being mentored. She seemed to believe that seeing people who "have done well" through an experience and hearing encouraging testimonies from them should bring reassurance for the new African student. What is it like to have someone with whom to share a sense of a potentially confusing experience that may lie ahead?

Binu described his school as a multi-cultural international institution. He said, for that reason, the faculty needed to be constantly equipped with information that would make them further sensitive to that fact. Funmi believed that such information would help faculty to remember that the students were from different backgrounds and to be more understanding and a little more patient."

The students described a vision of teachers who would demonstrate a genuine sensitivity to cultural differences not only in what they said but also in their manner and attitude of relating with students who were strangers in their new place of being. What is it like to experience a culturally sensitive teacher? What fosters learning in a culturally sensitive relationship?

BEING CHANGED

Time changes and changes human beings. Human experience is temporal and African students were aware of changes that had taken place in and for them over time. Over time, the students transitioned into the educational system of the U.S. but also the possibility of some definite transformations. The students increased in their mastery of their own lives, feeling of self-worth and in self-confidence. Being in the U. S. became for them a journey inward that awakens the development of whole vision and a new knowing. It was a new engagement with life itself, a second chance at meaning.

Abeke felt excited about her newly acquired sense of independence. She said, "Being here by myself, studying on my own and working makes me think I am doing something good by myself. I've been in school since 1994. I never failed a class. I feel good about myself. Now, I'm more independent. I'm proud of myself."

One significant transformation in this student was a new sense of self-confidence, independence, and a new feeling of self-worth. The student talked about the changes in the sense they would not have taken place if the student had remained in her familiar comfort zone back in Africa. What is it like to do well by oneself? What does it mean to be proud of one's self?

Looking back in time, Dayo, who had just completed her B.S. program at the time of our conversation said, "It seemed like a far off dream . . . but being able to not stop at all, being able to hang in there, it is now an amazing accomplishment." What a glorious and joyous sigh of relief! But more importantly she noticed a change in her own thought process and said, "I now look at things in a different light. I found myself being able to say, 'whatever I've learned that is new, where and how do they fit into the old? How does the old fit into the new?' It's like reconciling two worlds. Sometimes, they are reconcilable, sometimes, they are not."

The transformation experienced by Dayo was multi-layered: a new ability to look at life differently, a readiness to make meaning of a variety of experiences and awareness that some experiences might be unknowable, inexplicable or irreconcilable. The African students frequently found themselves trying to understand their American experience through previously created African lenses. At other moments, they are reconsidering familiar African practices through their newly developed American perspectives. Many of such moments were indeed, epiphanies; moments that leave marks on people's lives with great potentials for creating transformation; turning points after which one is never again quite the same.

Chapter Five

Concluding Thoughts

Being in the U.S. for African students was an opportunity to realize their individual dreams. For some it was an opportunity for further education or to learn from experts. For others, it was an opportunity for building "a good career" or an opportunity to join a spouse. In fact for some, it was an opportunity for realizing a combination of those dreams.

To dream is to imagine or believe a thing is possible, and picture it to oneself. In dreams, we regress both in content and in form into the primitive recesses of our minds where we draw on the vibrant language of the subconscious. We delve into the realm of the mind where contradictions abound, where the laws of objective reality are suspended, where the relationship between cause and effect is hazy and where past, present, and future are frequently fused into one and the same.

Being "something greatly desired" and tremendously powerful, the students' individual dreams soon became a tremendous source of energy and motivation for them to go through their experience in spite of the difficulties and challenges encountered. However, as the students became increasingly aware of aspects of the American social life and educational system that were unfamiliar, challenging or difficult, the subjectivity of their dreams came face-to-face with the stark reality of the challenges of realizing those dreams.

Constantly remembering that the opportunities that rendered the dreams realizable were either not available to many in their home countries, the students sustained their determination to endure the hardships on the road to their dreams. The past, the present and the future being one and the same in dreams, the students found the self of the present transforming the self of the past into the dreamed self of the future. It was the strength of this vision that provided the drive to leave home in spite of the pain of that detachment and to face the challenges of being a stranger.

Many of the experiences described by the African students speak to their being strange to others and finding others strange. They, their teachers and their peers have entered one another's interpersonal realms where they all, naturally, experience themselves as yet being apart from others. They live on that edge between their own unique world and the world of the others they have just entered. What opportunities for learning and caring open up as the faces meet at that edge? Each person has brought into the edge, their knowledge, sentiments, prejudices, biases, indeed their past and entire being that others may not know. This provides ground for exclusiveness, alienation and awkwardness through which strangers must live.

There are some elements that curriculum theorists should foster to make curriculum a jointly meaningful and transformative experience for the stranger and the others with whom they live. These include the ability to understand culture as historical, social, individual, and valuable; and a willingness to accept one's ignorance and to learn from relating to the horizons of "others".

Knowing, many times, leads to a form of confidence and a dangerous state of arrogance and closure. On the other hand, openness, intellectual humility and active listening help one to approach the other person with an attitude of understanding and caring. The other is allowed to be, and to be different, with respect and worth.

What do African, and possibly other foreign students, expect most from their teachers and American peers as they transition to a new culture and live out their dreams? Part of the answer can be found in Eniola's statement that, "Nobody understands where you are coming from." In the same light, Ruth described her experience as being in-between the American and her South African cultures. Similarly, Biola remarked that she could not totally relinquish her own (that is African) culture. If we keep our core values, what happens to growth? What part of one's past is lost when letting go is partial? What transformation is brought about for the students by values lost, by values kept and by new values developed?

Many schools institute programs to facilitate the experience of foreign students as they transition into education in the U.S. These programs include lessons in English as a foreign language, how to write term papers, and effectively take multiple-choice tests. Very few of the students used some of the programs. Insights gained from the experience of African students reveal that in spite of these programs, the students, their peers and teachers still confront the issue of not understanding one another on frequent occasions. An additional dimension of this issue is that, the students believe that if others 'try to understand' them, most likely they will.

Being a stranger is therefore a struggle with the new situation when the stranger has not grieved the old or the part of the old that has been given up or lost. So whether strangers have left a country, a tribe, a family, or the past, they will need to mourn the loss of the past. Strangers will never resolve their dilemma until they have grieved over what was and over what they thought was, so that they will not be projecting their idealized past into their present reality. In their new situations, strangers need to reaffirm the foundation of their pasts. They must decide what they need to relinquish and what sacrifice they are willing to make for subsequent adaptation. Sometimes, the price of success is letting go of the familiar. At other times, strangers live in between. They constantly remember that even though they now live in a foreign place, they will one day return home. So, they learn and try to practice what is culturally acceptable in the foreign place while they keep, and continually teach their children never to forget home values, for, sooner or later, they will need those values.

Being strangers, the students experienced some difficulties and challenges, some of which seemed to ease up with time. Early in their experience in the U.S., many students were lonely. For some, the sense of loneliness was so severe that it bordered on alienation. The students described loneliness as "trouble" or "one of the worst feelings that one can have." Although their peers gradually "warmed up" to them, the African students, being accustomed to instantaneous cheering up to strangers thought that the "warming up" was too slow. The consequent isolation and loneliness probably made the early part of the students' experience more stressful. However, the loneliness represented a call for the students to transition from a mindset of kinship, family and communalism to that of independence, individualism and autonomy. One wonders what assumptions about their being they had to confront or alter in order to make the transitions

Finding information and fending for one's self were other challenges encountered by the students. The students described the experience as "hard" and "difficult." The difficulty seemed to be compounded by the students not asking for information or for help and their unfamiliarity with going to school and working at the same time.

Differences in accents made it difficult for African students to understand and to be understood by others. The students also found it difficult to understand American metaphorical expressions. The difficulty led to frustration, embarrassment and feelings of inadequacy. Some of the students consequently lost voice by becoming silent. In contrast, others regained voice by requesting clarification of speech, including metaphors they did not understand.

Students discovered differences between African and American cultural practices that they needed to learn and to which they had to adjust. The experiences described by the students called them to a new cultural sensitivity with regards to touching, personal space, time, and a life of strict scheduling. In addition, the students discovered behaviors in the African context that did not necessarily hold the same meaning in the American cultural practice. For example, to look American teachers in the face or call them by their first names might signify disrespect. It took time for many students to recognize and adjust to those cultural differences.

Students experienced their first year at school as the most confusing and stressful. Abeke described it as being like a thunderstorm. It was faster in pace and broader in content than they had expected. On top of that, the student discovered it was pretty much an independent affair. The experience, however, had some growth promoting potentials. It awakened the students to the need to modify their reading styles and exercise their capacity for patience. They made more friends and walked more closely together with others who had just survived the "thunderstorm." What curricular practice can best help students go through their first year in school without losing the growth promoting potential of the confusion, briskness and breadth of a "thunderstorm" learning experience?

How does an African student brave the "thunderstorm? As the student becomes a stranger, clouds of storm begin to gather. The clouds collide, producing energy and gaining motion. Rain, thunder and lightening quickly develop, precipitating panic. The storm produces confusion and may become destructive. The student is also aware of the dangers of thunderbolts. Yet, the student braves the storm, as they remain alive. What do all these have to say about courage and the power of dreams? What does the lightening signify in the student's experience? Is it a godsend to light the path of the stranger in this unfamiliar road? Or, is it the awareness or illumination that one's life could be different? What is the darkness that precedes the lightening? Is it the self of the past awaiting transformation to the dreamed self of the future? What message is carried in the sound of thunder? Is that a reminder that power belongs in the student's voice? Or, does it scare the students because it overshadows the call to care? There is a silence, a space, and interval, between lightning and thunder. What is that all about? What goes into that pause? Or is that "The pause before the shifting paradigm?" What are the winds of change in the storm? Are they sources of anxiety for the students? Does the student feel alone and disillusioned in the wind? Do the winds call for change in identity? What is the nature of an identity crisis that is brought on by one's own dreams and action? What is it like to have self-initiated change happen by an explosion of accumulated forces? What is it like to have a new way of viewing reality so full of tension, energy and the intimidation of cracking thunder? What is lived time like for a student in a thunderstorm? Is it a sudden unfolding bursts and blossoms of time as opposed to time that is linear, ordinary or steady? What is support-ive to the students in that time?

As the 'storm-bravers' came out of the thunderstorm through determina-tion, they discovered that their experience had been one of transformation. Some discovered that they had become more independent, some, more as-sertive and some found voices that once were lost or inaudible. For some, the change implied developing new ways of being and new ways of viewing reality. Teachers who understand diversity and the world of the foreign stu-dent can better foster and facilitate those development and transformation not only for the African students but also for other foreign students.

Objective testing and use of the computer were difficult to the students. Most of the students were familiar with the less technological African educa-tional system. They were used to the essay mode of testing. For the purpose of testing, therefore, the students had to transition from a mindset of descrip-tion and explanation to that of making discriminating judgments between op-tions. How can the students be helped to make the necessary transitions? Or, are the two mindsets reconcilable? How can the students' learning of the com-puter best be facilitated to aid schoolwork?

Students talked about various experiences during which they thought they were being judged by race, accent, or color. They described the experiences as frustrating and embarrassing. They used the words bias, prejudice, being stereo-typed, being underestimated and being discriminated against to describe their experiences. The stories narrated by the students cut across student to student, teacher to student, black group to white student group, and African American to African student relationships. Many of the experiences were emotionally laden. Some were so crucial that one student considered changing her name to sound American. Being different thus became a source of threat to self-identity, leading the student to consider sacrificing self-identity on the 'altar' of self-protection.

Stereotyping is a natural phenomenon by which all humans develop cate-gories to help make sense of their environment. We use stereotypes as pet for-mulas to simplify our problems and solve them as easily as possible. How-ever, such categorization has its down side; the broader the categories, the more inaccurate they are likely to be and the more they tend to minimize, disregard or even assault the individuality of the other person. This type of disregard or assault is likely to be the source of the pain reported by Dayo whose teacher addressed her as "you people." She was so upset, she cried.

What fosters sensitivity in teachers and students? If our individual preju-dices constitute the historical reality of our being, how can we use them to en-hance understanding of one another? Sometimes the interactions described by the students as racial discrimination were precipitated by mutual lack of understanding of each other's cultural differences between teacher and student. Cultural differences with regards to touching, personal space, respect and time led to incidents characterized as discrimination or prejudice by the students described in this book.

Sometimes teachers misunderstand their students' cultural behavioral styles and under-estimate their intellectual potentials. They unknowingly mislabel and mistreat their students. They may underestimate their students' cognitive abilities, academic potentials and other skills. Consequently, they may oversimplify or over-concretize teaching, thereby slowing the student's pace of learning. While the teacher is doing all that, the affected students are increasingly being alienated from the teacher and from participating fully in the learning activities. At the same time the teachers may continually wonder why the students in question are not doing well.

Although prejudice and ethnocentrism seem to be part of the human condition, teachers should be less prejudiced and ethnocentric than the average person. Most students in every ethnic group can achieve the basic requirements in school under the proper conditions. In most U.S. urban schools, students, teachers, and administrators lack helpful guidelines to establish good race relations and foster academic achievement among minority and nonminority students. There are many teachers who get entangled in issues of racial discrimination simply for lack of knowledge and skill for confronting racially sensitive encounters. How could teachers be prepared to encounter cultural and individual differences? How could culturally sensitive communities be fostered among teachers and students?

There is a need for fostering cultural sensitivity in schools most especially because of its effect on self-identity. Negative self-image is a common consequence of prejudice and discrimination. Continual treatment as an inferior encourages a loss of self-confidence. If everything about a person's position and experiences works to destroy pride and hope, that person may become apathetic. What do students learn when their confidence and self-identity are threatened? What strategies can be adopted to minimize prejudice and discrimination in schools?

Dialogue groups have emerged as an effective means of challenging the prevailing institutional climate on college campuses that poses serious limitations for positive inter group interactions among students of different social cultural backgrounds. The dialogues provide opportunities for breaking down racial barriers, challenging the ignorance inside and outside oneself and gaining new insights, new connections and new identities. Dialogues serve as a means for engaging new questions and building coalitions for new possibilities. There are people who suggest that teachers should be able to rise above difference. That may not be any easier than telling a depressed person to "shake it off." There is a need for caution not to trivialize real lived experiences. Teachers need to be equipped to understand difference and use it for socially positive outcomes. Furthermore, equating all differences can leave individuals feeling devalued. The issue in most racial and ethnic episodes is not that students want to experience equality from teachers. Rather, they are calling for an attitude of fairness and caring in spite of whatever differences there may be.

Students became increasingly stronger in confronting the challenges they encountered as strangers. This gradual transformation was aided and strengthened by the students' tremendous value for education, strong determination to succeed and instructors, friends and family members who were caring. The students described people that were caring as those who "listened," those who "were accommodating" and those who were "encouraging." What is it about listening that makes it caring? There is a "staying with" dimension needed to listen long enough to develop familiarity and intimacy to what is being heard. By making spaces for listening, therefore, we nurture the sense of relationship and responsibility. We engage in what is truly an ethical and moral caring practice. We foster the making of the strange familiar and intimate.

It is often the face of the other that compels one to respond and to enter into an ethical caring relationship with the other. The face calls us to care, to protect what is vulnerable, to seek to prevent hurt and to heal what is broken. It places a burden on us to strengthen what is good, to enhance what is unique, and even to sponsor personal growth in the other. Most times, all these can be done by the compulsion of the face of the other accompanied by a speech climate that is personal, one that does not conform to any rigid rules. When Binu's teachers say "hi," they created a personal and relational speech climate; when they said, "to forget the past," they were using tactful action to heal what was broken, and when they were "accommodating", they must have created a speech climate that did not conform to rigid, set rules but one that opened up meaningful and gainful dialogue. The academic environment should seek ways by which it could foster such a speech climate in schools.

Chapter Six

Now, What?

Both teachers and students need to seek to understand one another through open-mindedness. This becomes even more necessary when teachers relate to African and other foreign students who are transitioning as strangers into the American culture. Teachers, being the ones with tremendous power, need to initiate the process of mutual seeking to know one another. This mutual seeking presupposes that both the teacher and the student do not know each other and are not assuming that they do. Yet, each sees the other as valuable to his or her success and the success of their relationship. Each is open to respect the other. The teacher begins the process with a stance of open-mindedness to differences, the cherishing of diversity and the development of a consciousness for the historicity of being. This makes the teacher's power, transforming power, the type that fosters self-worth and self-confidence in the student and opens doors for the teacher to reach the inner recesses from where, many times, the student can best be helped.

African students need to reflect carefully on the memories of their home, family and past to which they still feel bound and connected. They need to uncover the meanings this bounding holds for them and consider which ones are nourishing and which ones are limiting to their present experience.

Teachers and peers of African students need to show more understanding of the struggling that may be going on in the minds of the African students while transitioning in-between cultures. They need to show understanding that the frequent reference to home and Africa, and the occasional awkwardness may be part of their grieving of the past and transition into the present.

When the face of the African student beamed with joy because another person "warmed up" to her, the experience signified acceptance to the student. When a student said "listen and try to understand me," it was a call to the other person to show understanding to student's challenging experience of being a stranger. When Biola remarked that students grouped together for class assignments according to skin color, fear of detachment from people's comfort zones was conspicuously present in both groups. Teachers must constantly find ways to diminish racial prejudice and foster mutual inclusiveness in classroom settings

The stranger lives with a feeling of not belonging, of being different, of having lost a sense of self. How the academic community responds to the stranger will either alienate one from the other or will nourish insight, understanding and even peace. How then can we in the teaching and helping professions develop sensitive, caring relationships with those who feel set apart? We must always remember that we meet first as persons with varying backgrounds and with perhaps little information about the history and culture from which the others in the groups have come.

School should make recruitment and retention of minority and foreign students part of their goals and priorities. Teachers should not leave the advisement of the students to chance but rather initiate and develop relationships with students of color. Teachers need to be open, pay attention to the indirect relational messages that students may be sending them, and privately reach out to the students who appear to be withdrawing. In many instances, what the student is looking for is just some visible signs that the professor cares about, and is interested in, his or her well-being and success. Meetings and dialogues foster a sense of inclusion. They ensure that two people who are strange to each other know enough of one another to understand how each is experiencing a shared event. This calls on the teacher to initiate meetings and dialogues with their students, particularly strangers, students who do not participate in class, or who are doing poorly. To make meetings and dialogues more productive, teachers may encourage mutual sharing of personal and other stories. When we share stories from our lives, we begin to open ourselves to others, and perhaps nowhere are others more willing to come close enough to hear than when they are being told a story. Stories allow us to break through barriers and to share in another's experience; they warm us; they call us to attention. Through people's stories, we discover a variety of situations that make people feel either alienated or at home, while yet strangers. We hear the strangers' call more clearly and discover what they have to teach us.

Teachers and students need to develop an awareness of the increasing cultural diversity in universities. They need also to develop openness to difference along with that awareness. This might call teachers and students to an inward journey to explore their own presumptions and biases regarding sensitive relational issues of difference such as culture, diversity, caring, respect, language and family relatedness. It might require teachers to include in their busy schedules, the occasional reading of ethnic journals and the participation in some of the school's diversity promoting activities.

Teachers need to find ways to meet students especially those that seldom consult with faculty, remembering how much mutual insight and understanding could be gained through such meetings, dialogues and conversations. The creation of a speech climate might help protect what is vulnerable and unique in students. It may heal what is broken and strengthen what is good in them. It may enhance pedagogic relationships with students and among students.

Educational administrators need to design extra-curricular activities that bring students together more frequently as a way to promote diversity and enhance the students' appreciation of one another's difference and what they might learn from the difference. Administrators need to support faculty, morally and fiscally, in activities and training that enhance their sensitivity to cultural difference and diversity.

Prominent aspects of African students' experience were related to communication and the use of the computer. Technology has it merits and demerits. Because of its pervasive influence, it is vital that each individual learn about its nature and applications in order to gain the full benefits of its potentials and relate effectively to its power. Those who are computer illiterate will, in the future, be as helpless as those who are now unable to read and write. On the other hand, technology may alienate or intimidate students who are unfamiliar with it

Students told of how they were scared and intimidated by the computer. They expressed disappointment about peers who were too busy with the computer to care about them. African students need to take basic computer literacy classes as early as possible in their programs, realizing the difference this could make in their learning experience. How is a teacher called to be with students whose teaching and learning are being impeded by technology, communication and the computer? What challenges and claims does African students' difficulty with technology make on administrators? What might African students themselves do to minimize their difficulties with the computer?

African students told stories of how communication became a handicap because of fear of being mocked or underestimated, or the possibility of not being understood. Teachers and other students need to communicate their inability to understand a foreign accent in a caring manner; one that shows genuine desire to understand and value whatever the students want to communicate.

African students need to develop the attitude of asking questions, seeking information and seeking help. They need to learn these habits as early as possible in their experience because such learning influences the direction, nature, and success of their later experience as it unfolds. Teachers, administrators and the students' senior peers should encourage and assist the students in learning the said habits.

African students need to prepare their minds more to encounter different cultural norms and values and ways of being. Particularly, they need to learn early in their experience the value placed on timeliness and be open to differences in the meaning of respect and other cultural practices in the American culture. They need to be ready for an instant "curricular race" as soon as the semester opens so that at least the first year will not be experienced as such a severe "thunderstorm."

African students should take more advantage of faculty availability for consultation that characterizes the American educational system. They should consult more frequently with their teachers and advisors to create the familiarity that would enhance a growth promoting "speech climate."

African students need to take more and early advantage of any special programs instituted by the universities for foreign students to get acquainted with the computer, interpersonal communication, and formal paper writing. Some universities have programs such as the Big-brother-big-sister program under which they pair incoming students with more senior students to facilitate the orientation of the new students. The senior students should encourage the new ones to take advantage of the special programs mentioned above.

Curriculum can be seen as leaving home and leaving home can be seen as a form of curriculum. Detachment is the precursor to the birth of a new life, a vehicle for growth and continuous renewal. New growth and renewal occurred for the African students following detachment from their home-places. Leaving home was a way to recommence, to embark again, and to search for passages toward other ways of being in the world; other ways that would allow life to flourish. Leaving home fostered in the students, new ways of thinking and living. In what other ways can we use detachment carefully and responsibly? What do we learn about caring for ourselves, being detached? How do we achieve such learning?

The road to human development is paved with renunciation. Throughout our life we grow by giving up. We give up some of our deepest attachments to others. We give up certain cherished parts of ourselves. In other words, one does not achieve growth or renewal without giving up something. The giving up often involves what was once a treasured part of self. It is often painful and sometimes calls for grieving. Yet in it lies the uttermost possibility for growth and transformation.

African students need to develop a new sensitivity to relational behaviors such as punctuality, respect, care, personal space and touching. This will facilitate their experience and success especially in practical settings. They need to be attentive to people's reaction to their behaviors with a mind that is ready to learn what cultural differences mean and what is being signaled to them in various relational encounters.

The students need to be aware that strict adherence to time schedules will be expected of them in school and practical work settings while the more leisurely sense of African time might be disruptive to others with whom they work. The students need to consciously respect others' personal spaces and learn when and how to use touching for culturally acceptable purposes. Managers and supervisors need to be alerted, through continuing education programs, of varieties of cultural and individual differences they could encounter from African and other foreign students. They need to learn how best to relate to those differences with fairness and caring.

In the quest for deeper understanding of the experience of African students, this book has opened up other questions for further dialogue. Some of the questions uncovered are scattered in previous parts of the book. Other questions that need to be explored and pondered upon are highlighted in this final part of the book.

What do the teachers need most to know about strangers, their past and being, in order to foster and optimize learning? How might open-mindedness be used to promote understanding between teacher and student in various learning contexts? What functions might dialogues and sharing of family stories serve in teacher-student relationships? How might the African students facilitate their own struggle with their past for effective transition and transformation? What is the source of the students' belief that others do not make effort to understand them? How might teachers make their caring for students more obvious? How might we originate and sustain dialogues and conversations that build an open and caring academic community? What might help a teacher create caring relationships in classroom settings in spite of differences in students' mastery of language and technology?

The following questions also call for further clarity. What is the relationship between African and African-American students like? What makes African students believe African Americans see them as having come to deprive them of their entitlements? What do African and African-American students need to understand of one another to celebrate the transforming nature of difference and the empowering nature of their common heritage? What programs being used in universities today adequately nourish the positive potentials of difference? What do students from Africa find helpful and facilitative to their life success? What practices and strategies do culturally sensitive teachers use in working with foreign students? What do other students say about the practices of faculty that demonstrate cultural sensitivity and faculty that do not? How might educators use flexibility and fluidity in practice to enrich students' individuality? How might teachers and administrators enrich the pre-admission experience of African students especially in the areas of communication, language, cultural diversity and the use of the computer and other types of technology? How might they support African students' adjustment to language and cultural norms through collaboration with other departments such as those of linguistics and international support services?

Dialogues with African students in this book have revealed the value for education, attachment to family and to home, faith in God and a yearning for community that characterize the world of African students. The book has provided beginning insights into the world of African students, into how they sustain their determination to succeed in spite of the overwhelming obstacles that language, technology, and a different cultural environment place in their paths.

Bibliography

Abram, D. *The Spell of the Sensuous*. New York: Vintage Books, 1996.

Abu-Saad, H., and J. Kayser-Jones. "Foreign Nursing Students in the USA: Problems in their Educational Experiences." *Journal of Advanced Nursing* 6, (1981): 397–403.

Abu-Saad, H., J. Kayser-Jones, and J. Tien. "Asian Nursing Students in the United States." *Journal of Nursing Education* 21, no. 7 (1982): 11–15.

Achterberg, J. "Between Lightening and Thunder: The Pause before the Shifting Paradigm." *Alternative Therapies* 4, no. 3 (1998): 62–66.

Ager, M. *Language Shock: Understanding the Culture of Conversation*. New York: William Morrow and Co., 1994.

Airini, A. "Climbing up to Check the Sky: Culture and Curriculum." *Journal of Curriculum Theorizing* 13, no.3 (1997): 22–27.

Akka, R.I. "The Middle Eastern Student on the American College Campus." *Journal of The American College Health Association* 15, no. 3 (1967): 251–254.

Atwood, D., and R. Stolorow. *Structure of Subjectivity*. New Jersey: Lawrence Erlburn Associates, 1984

Bauser, B.P., G. S. Jones, and T. Auletta. *Confronting Diversity Issues on Campus*. Thousand Oaks, CA: Sage, 1993

Benner, P. *From Novice to Expert*. Menlo Park, CA.: Addison-Wesley, 1984.

Berman, L. "Being Called to Care: Curricular Changes." In *Being Called to Care*, edited by M. Lashley, M. Neal, E. Slunt, L. Berman, and F. Hultgren. Albany, NY: State University of New York, 1994.

Bennett, C. *Multicultural Education*. Needham Heights, MA: Allyn & Bacon, 1995.

Bishop, A., and J. Scudder. *Nursing: The Practice of Caring*. New York: National League for Nursing Press, 1991.

Bollnow, O.F. "Lived Space. Universitas 5, no. 4 (1960): 31–39.

Brandhorst, M. "Bridges or Barriers to Success: The Nature of the Students' Experiences in Nursing." *Journal of Nursing Education* 21, no. 7 (1982): 38–41.

Buber, M. *Between Man and Man*. New York: Macmillan, 1965a.

Buber, M. *The Knowledge of Man*. New York: Macmillan, 1965b.

73

Caputo, J. "Hermeneutics as the Recovery of Man." In *Hermeneutics and Modern Philosophy*, edited by B. R. Wachterhauser. Albany, NY: State University of New York Press, 1986.

Carnegie Foundation for the Advancement of Teaching. *Campus Life in Search of Community*. Princeton, N.J.: Carnegie Foundation Press, 1990.

Cohen, M.Z., and A. Omery. (1994). "Schools of Phenomenology: Implications for Research. Pp. 136–156 in *Critical Issues in Qualitative Research*, edited by J.M. Morse. Thousand Oaks, CA: Sage, 1994.

Colling, C., and Y.C. Liu. "International Nurses' Experiences Seeking Graduate Education in the United States." *Journal of Nursing Education* 34, no. 4 (1995):162–166.

Conelly, D.M. *All Sickness is Homesickness*. Columbia, Md.: Center for Traditional Acupuncture, 1986.

Cooper, M. "The Intersection of Technology and Care in the I.C.U." *Advances in Nursing Science* 15, no. 3 (1993): 32.

Creswell, J. *Qualitative Inquiry and Research Design: Choosing among Five Traditions*. Thousand Oaks, CA: Sage, 1998.

Crow, K. "Multiculturalism and Pluralistic Thought in Nursing Education: Native American Worldview and the Nursing Academic Worldview." *Journal of Nursing Education* 32, no. 5 (1993): 196–204.

De Luca, E. "Crossing Cultures: The Lived Experience of Jordanian Students in Nursing. Unpublished Doctoral Dissertation." *University of Maryland, College Park*, 1996.

Denzin, N.K. *Interpretive Interactionism*. London: Sage, 1989.

De Tornyay, R. "Creating Community among Nurse Educators. In *Community Building and Activism*, edited by NLN. NY: NLN Press, 1991.

De Tornyay, R. and M. Thompson, *Strategies for Teaching Nursing*. Albany, NY: Delmar Publishers, 1987.

Diekelmann, N.L. (1989). "The Nursing Curriculum: Lived Experiences of Students. In *Curriculum revolution: Reconceptualizing Nursing Education*, edited by NLN. NY: National League of Nursing Press, 1989.

Diekelmann, N.L. "Learning as Testing: A Heideggerian Hermeneutical Analysis of the Lived Experiences of Students and Teachers in Nursing." *Advances in Nursing Science* 14, no. 3 (1993): 72–83.

Diekelmann, N.L. (1992). "Behavior Pedagogy: A Heideggerian Hermeneutical Analysis of the Lived Experiences of Students and Teachers in Baccalaureate Nursing Education." *Journal of Nursing Education* 32, no. 6 (1992): 254–250.

Dilthey, W. *Poetry and Experience: Selected Works* 5, Princeton, NJ: Princeton University Press, 1985.

Dreyfus, H. *Being-in-the-world: A Commentary on the Heidegger's Being and Time*. Cambridge, MA: MIT Press, 1991.

Dukes, S. "Phenomenological Methodology in the Human Sciences." *Journal of Religion and Health* 23, no. 3 (1984): 197–203.

Edgerton, S.H. *Translating the Curriculum: Multiculturalism into Cultural Studies*. New York: Routledge, 1996.

Eliot, T.S. *Little Gidding: The Complete Poems and Plays of T. S. Eliot*. New York: Harcourt, Brace and company, 1952.

Ellsworth, E. "Why Doesn't this Feel Empowering?: Working Through the Repressive Myths of Critical Pedagogy." In *The Education Feminism Reader*, edited by L. Stone. New York: Routledge, 1994.

Englehardt, V. "Nursing Ethics in an Age of Controversy...Care vs. Cure." *Advances in Nursing Science* 9, no. 3 (1987): 34–43.

Eposito, L. "Care from Abroad." *Nursing Spectrum* 7, no. 18 (1997): 3.

Erlandson, D.A., E. L. Harris, B. L. Skipper, and S. D. Allen. *Doing Naturalistic Inquiry: A Guide to Methods*. London: Sage, 1993.

Femea, P., C. Gaines, D. Braithwaite, and V. Abdur-Rahman. "Sociodemographic and Academic Characteristics of Linguistically Diverse Nursing Students in a Baccalaureate Degree Nursing Program." *Journal of Multi-Cultural Nursing* 1, no. 1 (1994): 6–10.

Fergusson, M. *The Aquarium Conspiracy: Personal and Social Transformation in our Time*. New York: J.P. Tarcher, 1987.

Fuhrmann, B.S. and J. Grasha. *A Practical Handbook for College Teachers*. Boston: Little, Brown and company, 1983.

Gadamer, H.G. *Truth and Method*. London: Sheel and Ward, 1975.

Gadamer, H.G. *Philosophical Hermeneutics, Education, and Transformation*. Berkeley: University of California Press, 1975.

Gadamer, H.G. *The Relevance of the Beautiful and Other Essays*. Cambridge, MA: Cambridge University Press, 1986.

Gallos, J.V., and V.J. Ramsey, *Teaching Diversity: Listening to the Soul, Speaking from the Heart*. San Fransisco: Jossey-Bass, 1997.

Goode, J. and J. Schneider. *Reshaping Ethnic and Racial Relations in Philadelphia*. Philadelphia: Temple University Press, 1995.

Grahame, K. *The Wind in the Willows*. London: Chancellor Press, 1987.

Greene, M. *Teacher as Stranger: Educational Philosophy for the Modern Age*. Belmont: Wadsworth, 1973.

Greene, M. "The Tensions and Passions of Caring." In *The Caring Imperative in Education*, edited by M. Leninger and J. Watson. New York: National League for Nurses, 1990.

Guba, S. and Y. S. Lincoln. *Fourth Generation Evaluation*. London: Sage, 1989

Hammond, M., J. Howarth, and R. Keat. *Understanding Phenomenology*. Oxford, UK: Basil Blackwell, 1991.

Heidegger, M. *Being and Time*. New York: Harper & Row, 1962.

Heidegger, M. *On Time and Being*. New York: Harper & Row, 1972.

Heidegger, M. *The Basic Problems of Phenomenology*. Bloomington: Indiana University Press, 1975.

Heidegger, M. *The Question Concerning Technology and Other Essays*. New York: Harper & Row, 1997

Heidegger, M. (1993). *Basic Writings*. New York: Harper Collins, 1993.

Hekman, S.J. "Action as Text: Gadamer's Hermeneutics and the Social Scientific Analysis of Action." *Journal of Theory of Social Behavior* 14, no. 3 (1984): 333–354.

Hezekiah, J. "Creating Bicultural Experiences in Nursing: Helping Students from Pakistan Adjust to Canadian Culture and Readjust to Their Home Culture." *Journal of Continuing Education in Nursing* 24, no. 6 (1993): 14–18.

Hillard, A.G. "Behavioral Style, Culture, and Teaching and Learning. *Journal of Negro Education* 61, no. 3 (1992): 373.

Hodgeman, C.H. "African Political Activities at an American University." *Journal of the American College Health Association* 17, no. 2 (1968): 119–125.

Holy Bible. *Ecclesiastes* 3:1–18. Walls, IA: World Bible Publishers, 1994.

Hoobler, D. and T. Hoobler. *Images across the Ages: African Portraits.* Austin, TX: RSVP Publishers, 1993.

Hooks, Bell. Talking Back: *Thinking Feminist, Thinking Black.* Boston: South End Press, 1989.

Huang, K. "Campus Mental Health: The Foreigners at Your Desk." *Journal of the American College Health Association* 25, no. 3 (1977): 216–219.

Hultgren, F.H. "Being Called by the Stories of Student Teachers: Dialogical Partners in the Journey of Teaching." Pp. 117–139 in *Alternative Modes of Inquiry in Home Economics,* edited by F.H. Hultgren and D.L. Cooner. Peoria, IL: Glencoe, 1989.

Hultgren, F.H. "Being called to Care." Pp. 94 in *Being Called to Care,* edited by M.E. Lashley, M. Neal, E. Shunt, L. Berman and F. Hultgren. Albany, N.Y: State University of New York Press, 1994.

Husserl, E. *The Crisis of European Sciences and Transcendental Phenomenology* Evanston, IL: Northwestern University Press, 1970.

Jasper, M.A. "Issues in Phenomenology for Researchers of Nursing." *Journal of Advanced Nursing* 19, (1994): 309–314.

Johnson, S. In *Familiar Quotations,* edited by John Barlett. Boston: Little, Brown & Co., 1980.

Kayser-Jones, J., and H. Abu-Saad. "Loneliness: Its Relationship to the Educational Experience of International Nursing Students in the United Sates." *Western Journal of Nursing Research* 4, no. 3 (1982): 302–315.

Kayser-Jones, J., H. Abu-Saad, and N. Akinnaso. "Nigeria: The Land, Its People, and Health Care." *Journal of Nursing Education* 21, no. 7 (1982): 32–37.

Kavanagh, K., and P. Kennedy. *Promoting Cultural Diversity: Strategies for Health Care Professionals.* Thousand Oaks, CA: Sage, 1992.

Keane, M. "Preferred Learning Styles and Study Strategies in a Linguistically Diverse Baccalaureate Nursing Student Population." *Journal of Nursing Education* 32, no. 5 (1993): 214–221.

Kearney, R. *Dialogues with Contemporary Continental Thinkers: The Phenomenological Heritage.* Dover, NH: Manchester University Press, 1984.

Kincheloe, J. and W. Pinar. *Curriculum as Social Psychoanalysis: The Significance of Place.* Albany: State University of New York Press, 1991.

Kreisberg, S. *Transforming Power: Domination, Empowerment, and Education.* Albany: State University of New York Press, 1992.

Kurtz, J.M. "The Adult English-as-a second-language Baccalaureate Nursing Student." *Journal of Nursing Education* 32, no. 5 (1993): 227–229.

Lagrand, L.E. *Changing Patterns of Human Existence: Assumptions, Beliefs, and Copying with the Stress of Change.* Springfield, IL: Charles C. Thomas Publisher, 1988.

Lashley, M., M. Neal, E. Slunt, L. Berman, and F. Hultgren. *Being Called to Care.* Albany: State University of New York Press, 1994.

Lausteau, A. "Diversity and Challenge in our Student Body: English as a Second Language." Journal of Nursing Education 25, no. 3 (1986): 93.

Leonard, V. "A Heidggerian Phenomenological Perspective on the Concept of the Person." *Advances in Nursing Science* 11, no. 4 (1989): 40–55.

Leone, L.P. "Orienting Nurses from other Countries to Graduate Education in the United States." *Journal of Nursing Education* 21, no. 7 (1982): 45–47.

Levin, D.M. *The Listening Self: Personal Growth, Social Change and the Closure of Metaphysics.* New York: Routledge, 1989.

Levinas, E. In *Dialogues with Contemporary Continental Thinkers: The Phenomenological Heritage*, edited by R. Kearney. Dover, NH: Manchester University Press, 1984.

Levinas, E. In *Collected Philosophical Papers*, edited by A. Lingis. Boston: Martinus Nijhoff, 1985.

Lewis, M. *Shame: The Exposed Self.* New York: The Free Press, 1992.

Locsin, R.C. "Machine Technologies and Caring." *Nursing Image* 27, 3 (1995): 201.

Lowman, J. *Mastering the Techniques of Teaching.* San Fransisco: Jossey-Bass, 1984.

Martusewitcz, R.A. "Leaving Home: Curriculum as Translation." *Journal of Curriculum Theorizing* 13, no. 3 (1997): 13–17.

Mastorf, D.S. "The Relationship between Adjusting, Health, and Perception of Care in Two Groups of Cross-cultural Student Migrants." *Unpublished Doctoral Dissertation.* University of Pittsburgh, Pennsylvania, 1991.

Manhole, P.L. "Unknowing: Toward Another Pattern of Knowing in Nursing." *Nursing Outlook* 41, no. 3, (1993): 125–128.

Marchesani, L. and M. Adams. "Dynamics of Diversity in the Teaching-learning Process: A Faculty Development Model for Analysis and Action." *In Promoting Diversity in College Classrooms: Innovative Response for the Curriculum, Faculty, and Institutions*, edited by M. Adams. San Francisco: Jossey-Bass, 1993.

Moore, T. *Care of the Soul.* New York: Harper Perennial, 1994.

Morgan, G. *Beyond Method.* Beverly Hills: Sage Publications, 1983.

Mullen, C. A. "Narrative Exploration of the Self I Dream." *Curriculum Studies* 26, no. 3 (1994): 253–263.

Munhall, P. *Revisioning Phenomenology: Health and Nursing Science Research.* New York: National League for Nursing Press, 1994.

Napier, N.J. "Living Our Stories: Discovering and Replacing Limiting Family Myths." In *Sacred Stories: A Celebration of the Power of Stories to Transform and Heal*, edited by C. Simpkinson and A. Simpkinson. San Francisco: Harper, 1993.

Nathanson, D.N. *Shame and Pride.* New York: W.W. Norton Co., 1992.

Neal, M.T. "A Room with a View: Uncovering the Essence of the Student Experience in a Clinical Setting." *Unpublished Doctoral Dissertation*, University of Maryland, College Park, 1988.

Nehls, N. "Narrative Pedagogy: Rethinking Nursing Education." *Journal of Nursing Education* 34, 5 (1995): 204–210.

Oberg, A. and C. Blades. "The Spoken and the Unspoken: The Story of an Educator." *Phenomenology and Pedagogy* 8, (1990): 161.

Ollivier, J. *The Wisdom of African Mythology.* Largo, FL: Top of the Mountain Publishing, 1994.

Owhonda, J. *Nigeria: A Nation of Many Peoples*. Parsippanny, NJ: Dillan Press, 1998.
  Oxford English Dictionary I-X, London: Oxford University Press, 1933.
Paley, V.G. *White teacher*. Cambridge, MA: Harvard University Press, 1989.
Parillo, Vincent. *Strangers to These Shores: Race and Ethnic Relations in the United
  Sates*. New York: Macmillian, 1990.
Parry, A. "A Universe of Stories." *Family Process* 30, no. 3 (1991): 9.
Paterson, J. and L. Zderad. *Humanistic Nursing*. New York: John Wiley and Sons,
  1976
Phillips, S., and J. T. Hartley. "Teaching Students for whom English is a Second Lan-
  guage." *Nurse Educator 15*, no. 5 (Sept-Oct.1990): 29– 32.
Pinar, W. "Currere: Toward Reconceptualizatuion." In *Curriculum Theorizing: The
  Reconceptualists,* edited by William Pianr. Berkley: McCutchan, 1975.
Pinar, W., W. Reynolds, P. Slatery, and P. Tanbum P. *Understanding Curriculum: An
  Introductory to the Study of Historical and Contemporary Curriculum Discourses*.
  New York: Peter Lang, 1995.
Pipes, L. "Getting Started with Microcomputers." *Instructional Innovators* 25, no. 6
(1980): 10–11. Prema, T.P. "An Indian Psychiatric Nurses in the United States." *Nurs-
  ing Journal of India* 77, no. 8(1986): 208–222.
Ray, M. "Phenomenological Method for Nursing Research." Pp. 173–179 in
  The Nursing Profession: Turning Points, edited by P. Chaska. St. Louis, Mo:
  C.V. Mosby, 1990.
Ray, M. "The Richness of Phenomenology: Philosophic, Theoretic, and Mythological
  Concerns. Pp. 117–133 in *Critical Issues in Qualitative Research Methods*, edited
  by J. Morse. Thousand Oaks, CA: Sage, 1994.
Reeder, F. "Hermeneutics." Pp. 193–238 in *Paths to Knowledge: Innovative Research
  Methods for Nursing*, edited by B. Sarter. New York: National League for Nursing,
  1988.
Reinharz, S. *Phenomenology as a Dynamic Process: Phenomenology and Pedagogy*
  1, no. 1 (1983): 77–79.
Ricoeur, P. "Hermeneutics and the Human Sciences." Cambridge, MA: Cambridge
  University Press, 1981.
Rodriguez, R. *Hunger of Memory: The Education of Richard Rodriguez*. Toronto, On-
  tario, Canada: Bantam, 1982.
Rosen, H. "The Importance of Story." *Language Arts* 63, no. 3 (1986): 226–237.
Sartre, J.P. *Being and Nothingness*. New York: Philosophical Library, 1956.
Schubert, W.H. "Teacher Lore: A Basis for Understanding Praxis." In *Stories that
  Lives Tell*, edited by Carol Witherell and Nel Noddings. New York: Teachers Col-
  lege Press, 1991.
Schutz, A. *On Phenomenology and Social Relations*. Chicago: University of Chicago
  Press, 1975.
Sennhauser, S. "Psychological Nursing Intervention: A Vehicle for the Prevention of
  Illness among International Students." *International Nursing Review* 32, no. 6
  (1985): 176–177.
Serres, M. Rome: *Le Livre des Fondations. Paris*. Edition Grasset et Fasquelle, 1983.

Shabatay, V. "The Stranger's Story." Pp. 136–152 in *Stories that Lives Tell*, edited by Wthrell and N. Noddings New York: Teachers College Press. 1991.

Sharif, B.A. "Discussing the Needs of a Neglected Population: Adjustment Problems and Health Issues of International Students. *Journal of Health Education* 25, no. 5 (1994): 260–265.

Sinclaire, C. *Looking for Home: A Phenomenological Study of Home in the Classroom*. Albany: State University of New York Press, 1994.

Sisca, J.R., and J. Kerr. "Passing the State Board Examination: The Foreign Educated" Student. Journal of Nursing Education 23, no. 8 (1984): 358–361.

Slunt, T. D. "Living the Call Authentically." In *Being Called to Care*, edited by M. Lashley, M. Neal, E. Slunt, L. Berman, and F. Hultgren. Albany: State University of New York Press, 1994.

Smith, D.G. "The Geographic of Theory and the Pedagogy of Place." *Journal of Curriculum Theorizing* 13, no. 3 (1997) 3.

Smith, R. "Self Perceived Health Status and Conditions of International Students Enrolled in Intensive English Programs at SIU-C." *Unpublished Doctoral Dissertation*, Southern Illinois University, 1980.

Somé, M. *Of Water and Spirit*. New York: Harper Collins, 1994.

Soyinka, Wole. *The Open Sore of a Continent: A Personal Narrative of the Nigerian Crisis*. London: Oxford University Press, 1996.

Spiegelberg, H. *The Phenomenologic Movement: A Historic Introduction*, The Hague: Martinus Nijhoff, 1982.

Stapleton, T. *Husserl and Heidegger: The Questions of the Phenomenological Beginnings*. Albany NY: State University of New York Press, 1983.

Stein, H. "Culture Change, Symbolic Object Loss, and Restitutional Process." *Psychoanalysis and Contemporary Thought* 8, (1985): 301–332.

Stevens, W. "Thirteen Ways of Looking at a Blackbird." In *The Palm at the End of the Mind*, edited by H. Stevens. New York: Vintage Books, 1990

Strauss, A. *Mirrors and Masks: The Search for Identity*. Glencoe, IL: Free Press, 1959.

Tall, D. *From Where we Stand: Recovering a Sense of Place*. New York: Alfred Knopf, 1993.

Thompson, J. *Critical Hermeneutics: A Study in the Thought of Paul Ricoeur and Jurgen Habermas*. New York: Cambridge University Press, 1981.

Tomkins, S.S. *Affect, Imagery, Consciousness. Vol. 2: The Negative Affects*. New York: Springer, 1963.

Torress, C.C. "Education and the Archeology of Consciousness." *Educational Theory* 44, 4 (1994): 419–445.

Tracy, Brian. *Maximum Achievement*. New York: Simon and Schuster, 1993.

Trandis, H.C. *Attitude and Attitude Change*. New York: John Wiley and Sons, 1971.

Van der Post, L. *Feather Fall*. New York: William Morrow and Company, 1994.

Van Manen, M. *Researching Lived Experience*. Albany NY: State University of New York Press, 1990.

Viorst, J. *Necessary Losses*. New York: Simon and Schuster, 1986.

Walters, A.J. "A Heideggerian Hermeneutic Study of the Practice of Critical Care Nurses." *Journal of Advanced Nursing* 22, (1995): 492–497.

Webster, N. Webster's Third International Dictionary, New York: Houghton and Company, 1961.

Weil, S. *Gravity and Grace.* London: Routledge, 1972.

Weil, S. *An Anthology.* NY: Weiderfeld & Nicholson, 1986.

Wheatly, M. *Leadership and New Science.* San Fransisco: Bernett Koehler Publishers, Inc, 1992.

Yi, Tuan. *Space and Place: The Perspective of Experience.* Minneapolis: University of Minnesota Press, 1977.

Ziniga, X. and B. Nagda, B. "Dialogue Groups: An Innovative Approach to Multicultural Learning." In *Multicultural Teaching in the University, edited by D.* Schoem, L. Frankel, X. Zuniga and E. Lewis. Westport, CT: Praeger, 1993.

www.ingramcontent.com/pod-product-compliance
Lightning Source LLC
Chambersburg PA
CBHW021823270326
41932CB00007B/313